GROWING IN CHRIST

Shaped in His Image

ALSO BY MOTHER RAPHAELA

Living in Christ: Essays on the Christian Life by an Orthodox Nun

Becoming Icons of Christ

Growing in Christ

SHAPED IN HIS IMAGE

Mother Raphaela (Wilkinson)

Foreword by
Frederica Mathewes-Green

ST VLADIMIR'S SEMINARY PRESS
CRESTWOOD, NEW YORK 10707

Library of Congress Cataloging-in-Publication Data

Raphaela, Mother.
    Growing in Christ : shaped in His image / Mother Raphaela Wilkinson ;
foreword by Frederica Mathewes-Green.
        p.   cm.
    ISBN 978-0-88141-253-6
    1. Spiritual life—Orthodox Eastern Church.   I. Title.
BX382.R345 2003
248.4'819—dc21

                                                    2003054768

COPYRIGHT © 2003
ST VLADIMIR'S SEMINARY PRESS
575 Scarsdale Rd, Crestwood, NY 10707
1-800-204-2665

ISBN 978-0-88141-253-6

PRINTED IN THE UNITED STATES OF AMERICA

CONTENTS

FOREWORD

*T*HERE IS LIVELY CURIOSITY about spiritual things these days; while a few years ago any mention of religion, particularly Christianity, was met with disdain, now spirituality is exotic and fashionable. The pop singer Madonna declares herself a follower of the ancient Jewish mystical path of Kabbalah, and actor-heartthrob Tom Cruise is a stalwart follower of the newly minted faith called Scientology.

Some people look for spiritual experiences in ancient religions, and others seek them in beliefs crafted the day before yesterday, and some just look deep into their bathroom mirror. Everyone is looking for God, and many are looking in the wrong places.

What can we do with those who arrive at the doorstep of Orthodox Christianity, asking for a word that will guide, enlighten, or intoxicate them? There is no better person to open that door than Mother Raphaela, whose approach to the spiritual life is consistently steady, practical, and uncompromisingly honest. With *Growing in Christ*, people who want to learn how to have thrilling mystical experiences, or who seek merely nice, vague religious platitudes, will encounter something quite different: direct, bracing words from one who has lived the monastic life for many years and understands both what it is to be human and what it is to be loved by a God beyond all our comprehension.

Take, for example, chapter 13, "Climbing the Spiritual Ladder." It would be easy to find contemporary spiritual best-sellers that describe prayer in misty, feathery terms that leave the reader with a gratifying sense of being "spiritual" without any corresponding change in their hearts or behavior. Instead, Mother Raphaela counsels that paying attention to God is the whole point of prayer. "Just to 'say prayers,' or 'use the Jesus prayer' in such a way that we are more aware of ourselves praying than of being in His presence, is a waste of energy." We should learn to give an "inward nod of the head" to the Lord no matter what else we are doing. It is not necessary to enjoy long, elaborate prayers; some people find these an impossible challenge to their concentration. Yet when unwanted thoughts pester, a short prayer or Psalm verse can be used "almost like a tennis racket" to bat away the unwanted distractions. I won't forget that tennis racket. It is an image typical of Mother Raphaela's frank and useful—we might almost say "demystifying"—approach to the spiritual life.

It seems certain that in years to come we will see more and more seekers knocking at the door of historic Orthodoxy. Some will be motivated by confused desires and spiritual thrill-seeking, but even some of these will also be sincerely moved by the Holy Spirit to seek something they cannot yet name. It will be our task to love them, discern wisely, and lead them with patience. It will be our temptation to mince words in order to keep their affection. Thanks be to God for Mother Raphaela, whose plainspoken wisdom is an example to us all.

—*Frederica Mathewes-Green*

QUESTIONS ON THE WEB

Delicate threads
hold together
    the web of life.
Threads that run through the universe,
broken so often
    by people's blindness;
    insensitivity.

Threads
that hold together
    if not the families of nations,
        then at least a Christian family,
        a monastery, a parish,
        a diocese, a national church,
        the worldwide communion of God's own people.

Threads of care and consideration.
Threads of speaking and sharing.
Threads of attentively listening and hearing.
Threads of openness and trust.
Threads of respecting the role and vocation of others.
Threads of common goals and tasks.
Threads of putting aside one's own ideas and desires
    so that a larger group may flourish.
Threads of laying down one's own life for one's friends.

And all of this
not in the abstract,
but lived concretely
      with others.

You say you love God:
How can you love God
      whom you have not seen
when you do not love your brother
      whom you see?

How can you prove that you love your brother
            if you cannot live with him?

How can you desire authority
      over your brother
when you have not been able
      to live under authority yourself?

How can you rule and govern
when you have not experienced
      being ruled and governed?

What do you mean
that you don't feel a call to asceticism,
      to the life of family or monasticism,
yet you have a vocation to speak, teach, and lead?

What are you saying?
Are you saying

that you are incapable
of sharing a home, sharing daily goals and tasks,
    heartaches, joys and sorrows,
    with a small group of people,
yet know that you can have leadership
    over many?

Are you saying
that you can guide others
    while you yourself cannot receive guidance?

Are you saying
that the small details of life
    need not be taken into consideration?
That one can be effective
    when one's inner life and personal habits
    are unexamined patches of weeds?
Effective in what way?
To work out one's own agenda in one's own way
    or to answer God's call
        to do His work
        in a godly way that serves others?

Is your life, like your Lord's,
    informed by times of solitude;
    times when fasting
        from noise and activity,
        as well as from food, drink, sex, and luxury,
    in the silence
        you turn to God in prayer?

Do you allow the fire
   of His presence and love
to enter your life,
to burn out the filth
and refine the gold of truth and beauty?

Do you allow Him
   to shine through you
with His life, word, love, purity and joy
or do people see
   only your opaque flesh
   doing efficiently
   the job you think is needed?

Are you saying
that you are not willing
to open to others your mind and heart,
to put aside to some degree
   your personal habits and desires
so that you can experience the closeness of others,
   the closeness of men, women, children, in all states of
      life,
   as love rather than annoyance?

Explain to me then,
   how your love is other than superficial?
   Or a matter of your own convenience?
Explain to me
   how Someone other than yourself
   is at the heart of your being?

Answer these questions
   so that I may know
whether you are willing yet
   to face life and death;
   judgment and mercy.

You say this is too much?
Then how dare you be
   in a position where you may deny others?
How dare you say
   you are one
   who represents your Lord?

Or is there another lord in your life
   that you have not told us about?

Chapter One

FOR LOVE OF THE BRETHREN
(1 Peter 3.8)

A COMMON THREAD seems to run through many of the conversations we have had with friends these days. Some of these friends are women who are wondering whether they may have a calling to the monastic life; others are friends who are married and/or already settled into a career; and others are those who simply don't know what they should be doing with their lives.

If we are honest, we can recognize a similar struggle in our own life. It is a struggle to have a life of our own, distinct and apart from others around us, whether these others be family members, fellow community members, or fellow workers. Often we may feel that the demands of life are far too great for us; that we cannot fulfill our obligations to others and still have time for ourselves, to "be" ourselves.

Yet if we see our life as our own private affair, that we can only be our true selves when we are doing what we alone want to do without the need to respond to the needs and demands of others, we have created a false sense of identity, far removed from the human ideal taught by our Lord: "You shall love your neighbor as yourself" (Mt 22.39), and St Paul: "We, though many, are one body in Christ, and individually members one of another" (Rom 12.5).

When we fall into this mode of thinking, we begin to feel that time spent with our family or community or fellow workers is time taken from our "real" life. Looking at it this way, when the demands of family, work, or community encroach on more than just the edges of our life, we can feel real stress and anxiety. The energy needed to maintain a separate sense of identity while living in a close family or community environment can become phenomenal. In fact, those who enter into marriage or monastic life with such an attitude usually come to find themselves in a living hell. They cannot maintain this approach to their personal life and remain married or persevere as a member of a monastery.

For some people, there is an easy and quick way out of such a hell. They can withdraw from the demands of community and family, especially on a live-in basis. Such people often try to find a place to live and a means of support that will not take much time or energy from their perceived real lives. A simple job with undemanding hours, where even during their work they can think, dream, and look forward to the hours of their lives off the job can bring them a sense of real relief. Sadly, however, by trying to save their own lives, they lose them. These people end up at best on the fringes of life, unable to share fully in the abundance of love.

There is another way for Christians. It is the way of concretely dying—laying down our individual lives out of love for the brethren—and then discovering that there is abundant life after such a death. Accepted and lived out in one way or another, this death to the old man is definitely at the heart of any vocation or call from Christ our God.

There are all sorts of "christs" being preached these days. The Church preaches Christ crucified, and His words to *all*, not just to His chosen disciples, were, "If any one would come after me, let him deny himself and take up his cross and follow me" (Mk 8.34).

Beginning with St Paul, the Church has taken this saying of the Lord to mean more than facing just external difficulties. It means struggling with our own inner fallen tendencies, sins, and limitations. For this reason, people who attempt to live as hermits because they would rather not be bothered by other people, even if they manage to find someone who will bless them and let them live attached to the Church, are not taken as a norm for canonized sanctity. On the contrary, the writings of the spiritual fathers and mothers of the Church are filled with examples of how these people are susceptible to the extremes of delusion.

There are people, such as St Mary of Egypt, whom God calls to an authentic life apart from others. When their call is from God and not just a following of their own desires, it seems to follow some intense experience with others, beyond which they need to grow. These people certainly do not live lives of ease and comfort; they adopt at times even extreme forms of self-denial. And when their solitude is interrupted, they welcome those who come to them with Christian love, as St Mary welcomed St Zossima and as St Seraphim called those who came to him "My Joy."

Few of us are given the call to love through such heroic self-abnegation. For most of us, following the path of family and community opens the doors to love and abundant self-denial. I have seen both married people and monastics who can be relaxed and enjoy each other's company during normal times together and who also can be calm, peaceful, and absorbed when in prayer together in church or at home, or in solitude. It seems to me that this is the gift of simplicity and integrity, the ability to be the same, no matter where we are and with whom we find ourselves.

When I was a novice in monastic life, and complained to an older nun that someone had knocked on my door during my quiet prayer time to ask for my help, she replied that the spirit of my prayer was the spirit that manifested itself when I was interrupted. She said that if I had been praying in the Spirit of Christ, I would have met that interruption with the calmness and joy with which I would want to meet Christ Himself. That really startled me. I had never considered that there could be other spirits in "my" prayer, but over the years, I have certainly tested her wisdom many, many times and found it to be true.

Obviously, each of us has different and God-given natural tendencies: Some of us are naturally introverts and find it easier to be alone; others are extroverts and are happiest in the midst of a group. The extremes of either of these tendencies can become unhealthy, however, and we need guidance to find a balance. In a monastery, for example, extroverts need to be taught to spend time alone in their rooms to learn that solitude will not destroy them, but as the classic monastic saying goes, their room will teach them everything. Introverts on the other hand need to learn that they aren't going to be destroyed when they leave their room and spend time and bond with others. They may lose their fantasy life, but they will be better and stronger people for that.

The basic truth for us all is that each of us has a calling from God. He alone made us and knows far better than we what we are capable of being and doing. He may use our natural tendencies to call us to a certain life or task, or He may call us beyond what we think our natural tendencies are to fulfill a destiny far different and greater than any we would have chosen for ourselves. Even the Lord felt a struggle between His human will and God's will: "If it be possible, let this cup pass from me. Nevertheless, not my will, but Yours be done" (Mt 26.39). When we trust Him, He can lead us out of our self-imposed limitations. When He so wills, He can heal the wounds and infirmities that cripple our souls, minds, and bodies, whether they have been inflicted by others or by ourselves.

Yet we cannot grow in this way or be healed by ourselves. The seal of sanctity on the life of St Mary of Egypt was her ability at the end of her life to allow St Zossima to see her as she was and to make her confession to him. She was called from a life of abusive relationships to extreme exile and then, at the end, back to a life of communion.

The way that Christ holds out will be unique for each one of us. Nevertheless, when it is an authentic way to the kingdom of His Father and not a path into our own world of delusion, there will always be an element of this communion, of this willingness to let others see us as we are and learn from them. The classic icon of the Ladder of Divine Ascent based on the book by St John Climacus shows elders and monastics who have even reached the highest rung of perfection yet who, nevertheless, fall headlong into hell. Why is this?

I think the outstanding danger for all of us is the sense that we are better than others; that there is no one good enough to help us along our way. Even professional athletes who fall into this thinking find themselves rapidly losing their ability to perform. How much more is this true of the Christian athlete! No matter what heights we may believe we have reached in our lives, we can always learn from others. We can always put ourselves back into training. At the beginning of our path we have to be more careful: St John Climacus tells us to test someone before we choose him or her as a guide to be sure we haven't mistaken a sick man for the doctor or an untrained sailor for the captain of the ship. We need to find someone who has experience we can learn from; someone we feel we can trust and to whom we are willing to hand over a certain control—not in the sense of having that other person live our life, but in the sense of "letting go" so we can get outside of our own experience and learn from another's. As we become more mature spiritually, we discover that we can learn from more and more people as our vision becomes clearer. We can focus on the good rather than on others' sins, faults, and limitations. We can begin to see Christ rather than the devil in our neighbor.

After death, each of us will see and be seen by God together with our brethren for all eternity. We have the chance now to prepare to like such a situation. The less we are willing to learn to live life fully and to love our brethren here, the more difficult it will be for us when our masks are taken away; when we can no longer hide behind our fig leaves. In fact, if we really do not want the fullness of life and love, the presence of God and the fire of His love, which burns out all that is impure and imperfect in each of us, will become for us the fire of hell. We can never get away from God's life and love. According to the teaching of the Church, to refuse to accept it, to insist on our own reality rather than His, is the unforgivable blasphemy against the Holy Spirit. All other sins—blasphemy against Christ and His Church, fornication, murder, slander, lies, covetousness, gluttony— will be forgiven and burned away as we accept God's love and life.

Let us choose life. Let us choose to love our brethren whom we can see that we may learn to love our God whom we have not seen (cf. 1 Jn 4.20).

Chapter Two

ZEAL, PIETY, AND SANCTITY

S OMETIMES THE WORLD seems to be divided into those who think being zealous, pious, and holy are good things, and those who think they violate every principle of healthy human behavior.

The dictionary tells us that piety comes from the Latin word *pius* meaning "good," which in English has come to mean devotion, especially toward religion. Our English word *zeal* comes from a Greek word meaning "to burn." A similar English word is *fervor,* which comes from the Latin rather than the Greek but basically implies the same thing: eagerness, devotion, ardor, passion, enthusiasm, eagerness, warmth, fire . . . all good things. Yet St Paul tells us (Rom 10.2) that even when zeal (or ardor) is rightly directed toward God, it also can be misguided. Then *sanctity*: Who can quarrel with sanctity? In English, the word comes from the same root as our word *sanity,* from the Latin meaning "wholeness," so that *holy* is a synonym.

In God's mercy I believe I have met saints, sanctified people. Not the people with obvious piety one sometimes encounters, but men and women who have given me a sense of God's presence and love. Not necessarily great ascetics, they sometimes have showed some apparently serious defects such as hot tempers or compulsive habits, or have such poor health that they cannot even keep a minimal fast. They have reminded me of St Paul who wrote: "Thanks be to God through Jesus Christ our Lord! So then, I of myself serve the law of God with my mind, but with my flesh I serve the law of sin" (Rom 7.25); and "to keep me from being too elated by the abundance of revelations, a thorn was given me in the flesh, a messenger of Satan, to harass me, to keep me from being too elated" (2 Cor 12.7).

God glorifies Himself in such people with other gifts: They may be outstanding founders, builders, and philanthropists, leaving behind churches, schools, and seminaries; or monasteries, hospitals, and orphanages; or teachers of the Church and teachers of children; healers of soul and body who have studied and used many of the tools of modern knowledge and science, yet have known that with all their work and study, it is God who has healed through those means; nuns whose obedience has not allowed them to be great ascetics, but whose love, joy, and freedom have made me feel that I was palpably in the presence of the living God; and men and women whose interest in others, whose love and care has been self-effacing, sacrificial, and life-giving. These people have left behind for others a heritage of love, compassion, and godliness that infinitely exceeds any material heritage of wealth or power.

Many of the ancients felt that a certain type of zeal and piety would not be possible for later generations. There is more than one story of monks from the desert in the early Christian centuries telling of the great ascetic feats of the elders, yet with the "punchline" that in the "latter days" those who have no such feats but maintain their faith will be deemed greater in the kingdom of heaven.

What is the reasoning behind the ascetic piety of the Church? Our faith, based on God's unique incarnation in Jesus Christ, proclaims the redemption of the whole man, body and soul. When Jesus Christ was raised from the dead, and when He ascended into heaven, He was not a disembodied spirit. We do not believe that we should despise our bodies as something intrinsically evil that we will be freed from at death. On the contrary, even after death, the bodies of Christians are treated with great respect, and the bodies of those who have been manifested as holy perform miracles of healing and are venerated as we venerate an icon, as vessels sanctified by and mediating the Holy Spirit.

As Christians, we cannot have a spirit or a spirituality that is separate from our entire being. To be Christians, we cannot use just our minds to think holy thoughts—rather, our entire being, beginning with our physical body, must partake of the Body and Blood of our incarnate Savior, and organically and mysteriously, becomes physically one with Him. And according to His gifts, our entire being—soul, mind, and body—may grow into a health that approaches the life of Adam before the Fall. This "holistic" and scriptural approach to life allows us to enter fully into the mystery of the Church. We may dare to say with St Paul, "we have the mind of Christ" (1 Cor 2.16) and that we will become one Body with Him (cf. Rom 12.15 and 1 Cor 6), and that ultimately, as St Peter tells us, we are to become partakers of the divine nature.

There are those who have been sanctified by God's grace in this lifetime: There is a very strong tradition that even the bodies as well as the souls of some of these people have been beyond death, following in the footsteps of Jesus. Enoch and Elijah were said not to have died, but to have been "taken" bodily into heaven (Gen 5.24 and 2 Kg 2.10–12). The Mother of God and the Beloved Disciple died and were buried, but their bodies were raised and were not found. With Christ, these are the first fruits of the Resurrection. Then there are the well-documented cases of saints, such as St Seraphim of Sarov, who in life were seen to shine with the light of the Transfiguration. Their bodies remain with us on this earth, but like the fathers of the monastery of the Kievan Caves, they may be preserved from corruption in death and continue to be sources of miracles and wonders.

We can try to practice some of the ascetic feats of the ancients—but can we do it as a response in love to God who has first loved us? Can our asceticism produce or grow out of the deep peace, the joyful tears, and lack of anger and judgment that the desert fathers insisted must be the context and fruits of any ascetical effort? St Isaac the Syrian, perhaps more than any other spiritual writer, extolled the life of the spiritual athlete in solitude. He was, nevertheless, insistent that if one sees oneself as better than any other person on this earth, then one's efforts are delusion rather than true virtue.

There are many forms of extreme asceticism, found in almost every culture and religion: extreme solitude; fasting for periods of time from all food and drink; abstaining at all times from oil and animal products, cooked or seasoned foods; complete sexual abstinence; keeping vigil and depriving oneself of sleep; standing in prayer rather than sitting; limiting one's reading or hearing to the Scriptures and lives and writings of the saints; refraining from all humor and laughter or from indulging one's senses in the sounds of music or the comfort and scents of oils and perfumes; avoiding cleanliness, and so on. We know from reading the lives of the saints that there have been traditions of monastic guides who have been experienced in such "toils" and, like expert athletic coaches and trainers, have been able to guide neophytes in these ways, gradually allowing them to take on those tasks that are appropriate for their age and their God-given abilities. When such tasks are appropriate from a Christian standpoint, they help to expose and then purge the roots of self-will and self-indulgence, anger, neurotic illness, and any of the other results of sin that keep our humanity bound and limited.

The gift of tears is traditionally seen as the link between such deeds, thoughts, and intentions and one's heart and "gut."

According to the ascetical fathers of the Church, beginning with the desert-dwellers of Egypt and on down through St John Climacus, St Symeon the New Theologian, and St Paisius Velichkovsky (who is closer to our own time), there has been a very clear teaching that if one's life and efforts before God have not brought the gift of weeping for one's own sins together with tears of compassion for all mankind and the whole of creation caught in the travail of the fallen universe (cf. Rom 8.19–23), one's life and efforts have been in vain. But it takes enormous discernment and effort for men and women to grow into a healthy mourning that is not morbid depression or despair, and especially here, a sensitive and experienced trainer is a necessity. Simply to cut out a sense of humor and the ability to laugh and smile at appropriate times and have tears stream down one's face may be a sign of pathology rather than of the deep and selfless love that can only be God's gift.

There must be discernment, which is not a private affair, with all of these forms of asceticism, and the recognition that if God does not give one the gifts or the providence (including guides and trainers) to exercise such asceticism in a spirit of love, joy, peace, and long-suffering, then one's gifts lie elsewhere.

When we cannot emulate such ascetic feats, we should not say they are of no value. Indeed, until the end of the world, there will always be men and women whose great, God-given love allows them to strive in these ways with love for all mankind and for all of creation, but it seems that in these days, especially, such people are truly hidden. We will not normally know about them. They will not appear on TV nor will they be plugged into the Internet. Such feats of asceticism are a gift from God to strengthen the spiritual network of prayer that holds the fragile web of creation together, and they do not need to be observed or given human approval to be operative. On the contrary, the more deeply hidden they are, the more sacrificial the life of the one given such gifts—and the more effective will be the outpouring of love through them.

Let us pray that even in our day some will be given the gift of such deep love and the effort that offers their entire being to God. But let us not presume to take such a gift to ourselves before it is the time. We may struggle to take the kingdom of God by violence, but let this struggle be in love and humility, not in pride and arrogance.

Chapter Three

A TIME TO BUILD

Even quiet, peaceful monasteries sometimes go through periods of intense activity. In truth, most monasteries, however calm an exterior they present to visitors, are inwardly bee-hives of activity. In addition to the hours of liturgical and personal prayer, monastics take very seriously St Paul's injunctions to the Thessalonians, "For even when we were with you, we gave you this command: If any one will not work, let him not eat" (2 Thess 3.10).

No matter how "angelic" the monastic life may be on this earth, the men and women who live it do need to eat. They follow in the footsteps of their incarnate God and Savior who ate and drank. As more than one person has put it: "If it was good enough for Him, it's good enough for me." We endeavor not to worry about how we will get the necessities of food, drink, clothing, and shelter. Like the lilies of the field, we trust that if we are living in response to the Lord's call and accepting the reality of His providence one day at a time, He will provide for our needs. Humanly, when we do find ourselves worry-ing from time to time, simple prayer comes in. We turn to the Lord, let go of the worries, and say: "Let Your will, not mine, be done."

Obviously, however, this does not mean sitting with our hands folded when we should be working and expecting our needs to be magically met. Nor can we expect a monastery building to rise for us

27

with the wave of a fairy godmother's wand. The miracles of Christ are not the cheap tricks of a magician. Rather, they are signs that manifest the love and healing already present by His grace in the lives of those He has touched. We see our monastery building as just such a miracle: Those of us who live here, those who visit, those who come for longer periods to pray and work, and those who may never come but rely on the power of God working through prayer here, all of us together are being used by God to build this monastery.

Reading the life of Starets Paisius Velichkovsky has comforted us. While on Mt Athos, before returning to Moldavia to begin his great reform of Slavic monasticism, his monks spent much time and energy in building. They were often criticized for working through the regular times of prayer, but until they were finished, it seemed they had little alternative. History also shows us instances of monasteries being founded by individuals with access to wealth, which have brought in monks and nuns from other monasteries who have not had to be involved directly in building or raising funds. Those of us called in the Lord's providence as monastics living in poverty with no personal funds, however, find ourselves likewise blessed to be part of a living miracle.

The autobiography of Abbess Thaisia, a late nineteenth-century Russian nun, has also been encouraging to us. She spent months away from her monastery, even going on foot and begging door-to-door in places like Moscow, to raise the funds to build her monastery and church. Tragically, this center for renewal in the Church was later destroyed by the Soviets. Abbess Thaisia's monastery, together with her grave, lies beneath many feet of water behind a dam. Was her work in vain? Would it have been better if she and her sisters had never built? We do not believe so. Here, we have no continuing city, and how much more tragic it would have been if the Soviets had found nothing Christian to destroy! Our monastery, like hers, may well not last on this earth until the Lord's Second Coming, but the life, the prayers, the love, and the sacrifice that are building it will be a memorial for all of us and our friends before God in eternity.

We share a traditional prayer that has taken on new meaning for us through this time: "Lord, I shall be very busy today. I may forget You; please don't forget me." We are in God's presence, whether we choose to acknowledge that fact or not.

The Preacher in Ecclesiastes tells us that "for everything there is a season, and a time for every matter under heaven: . . . a time to break down, and a time to build up."

We pray that through this time of both breaking down and building up we may learn empathy for all those who find themselves in similar circumstances of demanding activity in this busy world. May we grow in our awareness of God's presence, and may His blessing strengthen us to be and do only what He would have us be and do.

Chapter Four

THE KNOWLEDGE OF THE

GLORY OF GOD

*H*ow OFTEN THE WORD *glory* is used in the Bible! Isaiah saw the glory of God in a vision of "the Lord sitting upon a throne, high and lifted up." Daniel saw it in a vision of the Son of Man coming upon a cloud in glory. It was this same glory that Peter saw when he fell down at Jesus' feet and, like Isaiah, cried, "I am a sinful man, Lord." It was glory that transfigured St Stephen when, full of the Holy Spirit, he saw the heavens opened and the Son of Man standing at the right hand of God. Having seen that glory he could pray for forgiveness for the men who were killing him.

The image of God most of us hold as twenty-first-century Americans is not the God of glory. We aren't even sure what glory is. We have exchanged that vision of glory for a life where the highest goal is a second car, a swimming pool, and retirement in Florida near a golf course. Instead of making pilgrimages to holy places, we save up for a trip to Disney World. We have sold our birthright of glory for what is in truth just fun and games.

Alexander Solzhenitsyn's saying, "men have forgotten God," is well known. Our own experience tells us that this is profoundly true. Even those of us who profess Christianity and attend church regularly find ourselves living most of our lives as functional atheists. Our knee-jerk reaction to most of the difficult situations we face in our lives is not to turn to God first, to pray, to allow His will to manifest itself in our words and actions, but rather to jump in and try to play God ourselves. Only when we fall flat on our faces do we cry out to Him as a last resort. How often do we rage, or at least complain, if He does not rescue us at the last minute from our own follies? We would rather not learn from our mistakes, and we resent a God who would allow us to be taught that way.

We are becoming like the fish that swim for generations in the darkest parts of the ocean and finally lose the ability to see light. We no longer seem to have the eyes to see the glory of God. In times past, for many people, cities like Constantinople and Moscow were like Disney World is for us today: paradise on earth. Yet if we take our faith seriously, we know with the writer of the Letter to the Hebrews that "here we have no continuing city." The true glory of the cities of Byzantium and of holy Russia was that they pointed beyond themselves. They did not pretend to be the final word in joy. Rather they proclaimed to all who had the eyes to see: "Do you think that this is beautiful and wonderful? You should see God and the kingdom of heaven where beauty, wonder, and glory shine infinitely beyond what you see here!"

Our churches should be places where we worship God with such truth, beauty, and love that strangers who enter will say, "We saw such glory, that we did not know whether we were in heaven or on earth," and "Truly God is in this place."

This true glory, this glory of God, can be found likewise in the transformation of our lives. Let us take a look at St Peter. Like many of us, he is sometimes known for his ineptitude, his weakness, and even his denial of the man he knew as his friend and master as well as his God. Yet he allowed himself to be transformed. How humiliating, some of us would say. For in the book of Acts, Peter is preaching boldly. Do people give him credit and say: "Look at the great man, Peter! Look at the good preacher!"? No. People look at him, and remembering what he had been like, they say, "This man has been with Jesus of Nazareth."

Peter truly is transformed. He walks on water. He heals the sick. He preaches with power and speaks with persuasion. He lives by that same power that raised the cold and lifeless body of the Lord. He speaks by the same might that allowed his Lord to walk through closed doors and bring peace to His distraught disciples. St Peter gives his life for the glory that he saw ascend to the heavens and descend again in the power of the Holy Spirit, the glory that can transform all mortal flesh into the life of God.

St Paul was a young fanatic persecuting the first Christians until a blinding vision of the glory of God transformed his life. He, too, went on to be a powerful and tireless preacher, laying the groundwork for the Church of Christ.

Let us take an example closer to our own time. The Grand Duchess Elizabeth of Russia, who lived in just the last century, was on the surface just another popular, fashion-plate royal princess, touted by the press of her day as "the world's most beautiful woman." It is said that her marriage was not a happy one, and when it ended tragically, she gave away all of her precious clothes and jewels. She had caught the vision of glory. She gave her life and all she possessed to serve her God, her Church, and her people. She began an order of deaconesses: nursing sisters who went out to the worst slums and hovels of Moscow caring for the poor, the sick, and the dying. She led and transformed the lives of others by her own life, work, and example. The power and glory of God transformed her from a shy, retiring woman to the woman of power who more than once brought rioting Bolshevik mobs to their knees in Red Square. She gave her life for that glory, praying and singing hymns to God even at the end when she and her companions had been thrown down a mine shaft by Communist soldiers who threw in lighted grenades after them.

Do we see that glory? Are we willing to have our lives transformed to such standards? Or are we willing to accept substitutes? Are we willing to learn to be loving and forgiving—you and I, in *our* circumstances, in *our* daily lives? Are we willing to be faithful? To be joyful? To be peaceful?—even when it isn't easy, when we aren't feeling well, and things aren't going our way?

God can transform our lives. And He will, unless we insist on holding on to them and keeping them for ourselves. If we do insist on having total control in our lives, on trying to control the lives of those around us, this will lead only to death. When we let go and let God control our lives and accept His providence in every person and event that comes our way, then in deed and in truth we find life; we find divine self-control, and to us are given all the fruits of the Holy Spirit.

Then even we can dare to do great things for His glory, or rather, we will find that God is able to do great things in and through us. Perhaps then, seeing us and remembering what we had been like before, men will say: "This person has walked with Jesus of Nazareth."

Chapter Five

PREPARING FOR CHRIST

MANY OF US HAVE HEARD how terrible it is to celebrate Christmas. Certainly I agree that it is important to get past the commercialization of the feast. There are all kinds of theories about how to get around this: Keep the religious old calendar so we can have a pagan winter feast with our friends and then have a spiritual, Christian feast later. Or we can stay on the new calendar and give religious, pious gifts. Enthusiastic people have come up with all kinds of Orthodox Christian gimmicks and slogans to counteract the advertising that bombards us the minute summer shows any signs of cooling down. We even can give twice by buying from the charity of our choice.

I would like, however, to suggest another way to turn around this whole approach to Christmas. It may seem now as if I am just playing with words, but I have learned that sometimes the words we use say more about what we really think and feel than we realize.

Rather than thinking in terms of putting Christ into our Christmas, we may rather think in terms of putting ourselves, including our Christmas, into Christ, as the renowned twentieth-century Orthodox theologian Father Alexander Schmemann used to say. Jesus Christ is at the center of the universe, and we need to find ourselves in our relation to Him, not the other way around.

It really is a bit presumptuous of us when, in effect, we say to the Creator of heaven and earth: "In theory, I think that You have created me; the fact that I can speak, think, stand upright, breathe, and live is only because You made me and became human like me in order to redeem me. According to this same theory I profess to believe, You are greater than the greatest expanse of the universe and You are also able to penetrate and know intimately the smallest element of the smallest microorganism or mineral in the smallest speck of dust. My deepest thoughts and feelings about You merely tug at the thin outer edges of Your reality. Your life makes my lifetime appear to be a passing shadow.

"Still, in the universe we actually live in, this whole theory about who You are doesn't register. I am in the center of this real life of mine and on a day-to-day basis, I give You the space I think I want or need for You in my life. Christmas as I know it is a celebration that gets along very well without much reference to You.

"But I am willing to acknowledge Your existence on occasion and in the right company. I will allow You to be part of my Christmas within limits. (This is the 'Put Christ into Christmas' approach). I don't plan to give up any of my personal plans and social events, but I think this year I may have time to spend an hour or so with the Church that is called Your Body—unless someone else has plans for me. Or the weather is a little bad. I might have to make it to our in-laws' even if there is a storm, but after all, You are more understanding than they are. And really, on a day-to-day basis, You are not as important to me as they are."

Now we might say, "I wouldn't think that way." But in our heart of hearts, we know that when and if we do try to think any other way, we are or would be branded as religious fanatics or people who are hypocritical saints—since no one can be that good and anyone who appears to be a saint must really be a hypocrite.

Probably in working through all of this, the most important thing for us to ask ourselves is: "Who is this Christ?" Certainly those of us who call ourselves Christians should try to ask this question, if not every day, then at least during this period when we are officially preparing for the coming birth of Christ into this world.

"But who do you say that I am?" That was the question Jesus asked His friends when He walked this earth, and people obviously had all kinds of strange ideas about who He was. How we answer that question will make a big difference in deciding how we are going to live our lives.

Jesus, our Lord God and Savior, may be an interesting person we hear about primarily in church, and we may even have some strong feelings and thoughts about Him on occasion. But our Creator? The Love and the Life that makes it possible for us to be here, breathing and thinking at this moment? I think that if we are honest, we realize we can't identify with those concepts. We live with democracy, freedom, and material security. We don't know what it means to depend on anyone for anything. And we really don't have any sense that there is a reality outside of our daily life. Being created from nothing? Living in the face of eternity? These are not meaningful concepts to us. We even are able to forget most of the time the fact that we are going to die one day and face Christ, His reality, and His eternity. On occasion, a death that hits close to home may lift that curtain for us, but preparing daily to meet the Lord is not part of being a normal Orthodox Christian in our age. The fact that it was the center of life for centuries of Christians who have gone before us is just an interesting historical note.

Therefore, to behave as if life and death, God and eternity have meaning for us on a daily basis would be hypocrisy. Right?

Being a hypocrite has become one of the greatest sins in our society. It must be avoided at all costs. Of course, there is real hypocrisy, and avoiding it is a fine line we must walk. But what constitutes real hypocrisy is a big question in my mind. By some current definitions, if you are, for example, a mother with a child and that child has aggravated you to the point where you want to strangle it, if you refrain from doing so and allow your child to live another day, you are a hypocrite. It seems that a murderer has more honesty and integrity, and I have heard this argument used in favor of abortions.

I have trouble with this. Such a definition makes it impossible to set goals or aim for anything higher than we have already reached. Yet such a definition is very pervasive in our society. Teachers and employers often say how hard it is to get young people to learn a new subject or trade. If they don't already know it, it isn't "natural" to them. And anyone who would try to learn something they don't already know by doing it is something of a hypocrite. The graphic arts have been very badly affected by this, including our Church iconography. I have known of people who didn't know how to draw, yet rather than study with someone who does know how and could give pointers, they use a prayer formula, seeming to hope it would, like magic, change their bad drawing into a good icon. Other art forms seem to have become at best a type of therapeutic self-expression, and those of us beholding them from the outside may find ourselves questioning whether they serve any other function.

Certainly any attempt to live a life that could be identified as Christian has been severely undermined by this approach. You don't understand church services? They aren't meaningful to you? Asking questions, studying, spending time trying to learn about their intricacy and beauty is often called fanaticism or hypocrisy. Going to more of them to get used to them is even worse. A child may attend early morning soccer practice daily, but an early morning church service? Some Orthodox even seem to think that reading the Bible in order to place the scriptural lessons into a context so they make more sense is something only members of cults do.

But I suggest that this way of seeming "hypocrisy" may be the way we should walk. We need to learn to pray. We need to develop a relationship with our God. We need to begin even when we don't really know how. To keep ourselves honest, we can say, "God, if there is a God, reveal Yourself to me," or "God, I want to love You," or "Lord, I believe, help my unbelief." We need to struggle with not getting the kind of answers unconsciously we may expect from God. He always responds to our prayer, but being the best of parents, He doesn't always say yes. And sometimes His silence is very loud because He is telling us that we need to grow up and figure out or do something on our own.

If we begin to do this, to put ourselves into Christ, Christmas, along with very many other things, will cease to be a problem. We will want to use every way we can think of to celebrate the greatness of the coming of our God and Savior. We have so many ways to choose from, and they are all literally God-given. We have the beauty and solemn joy of church services; the sharing of life in eucharistic communion as well as at our family tables, all heightened by the preceding days of fasting. We can decorate our surroundings; prepare beautiful things; pay more attention to giving and receiving love, including giving presents if they are important to us and to those we love; sing our hearts out; discover the neighbors who have less than we do and share some of our bounty with them. You can add to the list. All of these ways of human celebration and more can be brought before Christ, can be "baptized." If some of our ways of celebration can't stand before Him—getting drunk and making life hell for our family, for example—then we had best learn to let go of them.

Let us think about this. What are the things in my daily life and in my celebrations at times such as Christmas that I can bring before the Lord? How can I prepare for Him? Would I be willing to have Him walk in the door of our church the way we do the services? Am I grateful that He lived as Jesus in first-century Palestine so there is no danger He could walk into my house on Christmas day? These are some of the questions we can put to ourselves as well as to our children. Certainly Christmas is one of the times we should remember Jesus' words that we must become as little children to inherit the kingdom of heaven.

So rejoice in the Lord. Look for the joy of a child's wonder. Celebrate the feast. And let this Christmas be the beginning of a whole re-orientation of our life around the center of reality: God has made us and redeemed us, and in preparing for the Christ child in the manger, we prepare to welcome all the Life and Love in the universe.

Chapter Six

VIRTUE IN CHRISTIAN LIFE

*T*HE LITURGICAL TEXTS of the Church tell us that Lent is given to us in order to help us increase in virtue. They say that virtue is for us the way to life: the way to make our own the mystery of the Cross of Christ, to enter into the Resurrection, and finally, to taste of the banquet table set for us in the kingdom of heaven.

But exactly what is virtue? The root of the word comes from the Latin word *vir*, meaning a grown male person, an adult man as opposed to a boy, a man of character and courage. We are still familiar with the term "virile," which also comes from this root. The Latin adjective *virtus* means first "manliness," then, by association, worth, courage, bravery.

The English dictionary defines *virtue* as "moral goodness, excellence, strength" (by the *virtue* of the Cross), and then, curiously, in a telling example of how words sometimes take on the opposite meaning they originally had, as "specifically female sexual purity."

It seems, though, that when you get down to the root of it, virtue means strength. I would also like to suggest that virtue is for adults. For the men, not the boys. For people who make their own choices and take responsibility for their own actions.

So how does this virtue enter into our lives? Here I feel that I can't speak for others, and I will try to share some of my own experiences.

When as a pretty rowdy teenager I began struggling with the idea that for some strange reason God wanted me to be a nun, the thought of my being virtuous was hysterical to my family and terrifying to me. Among other things, I was one of those teenagers who could never be without noise. They hadn't invented earphones yet, but I still managed to have a radio going full blast every minute. And that usually meant there was even more noise as people shouted at me to tone it down. I was scared to death of what I might hear if there were quiet.

Fortunately, I was introduced to a wise, old priest who managed the first stage of breaking me in. He started me out with five minutes a day, sitting quietly, preferably in the chapel of the university I was attending, saying: "God, I want to love You." And he insisted that I be at every service held there.

That was the beginning. I will make a very long story short by saying that since that remedial beginning, I have been taught much about myself in particular and how we are put together as human beings in general. I have learned that my ability to be virtuous is God-given, but almost hopelessly stunted and crippled by my being part of this fallen world.

The Lord has made us to be open to suggestion. If I go around saying to myself, "I'm bad . . . I can't do that . . . I feel lousy," it is no surprise to find that I begin to behave badly; that I feel defeated and sick. This is the root of the corruption we call vice, the opposite of virtue. Vice also comes from a Latin root, *vitio,* meaning to "damage," "injure," "corrupt," "spoil," or "mar." From that same root, we get the English word *vitiate,* which means "to weaken or make ineffective," "to contaminate," or "to pollute."

Vice is for wimps. It takes a grown man or woman with courage to truly assess what is going on in his or her own daily life and to begin to want the God-given life and strength we call virtue, which alone can overcome all the undermining and debilitating sin in the world.

Let us not underestimate how much in our life has been badly corrupted and needs to be turned around. Many people who would say they are afraid of hypnotism spend literally hours every day in what has been clinically described as a passive trance state in front of a television set, open to every influence and suggestion sent over the tube. We know that if young children are raised with the television as a baby sitter, it can be physically measured that some of their brain cells will not develop at a critical stage, and the children will have severe learning disabilities that may never be turned around. There is no virtue or strength here. There is only undermining programming so that you, like those children, will be less able to think your own thoughts and make your own choices; so that you will spend more, lust more, covet more, and lose the ability to know God and experience the kingdom of heaven.

Do we realize that our every word and action makes an enormous, eternal difference in the lives of others? Are these words and actions our own, or are we driven by the suggestions of others with less than virtuous agendas?

Before Great Lent begins each year, we sing the liturgical texts for the Sunday of the Last Judgment. That is a terrifying service precisely because it is such a strong dose of reality. For Christians, our Lord God and Savior Jesus Christ is not just the warm, fuzzy, white light we will meet someday at the end of a tunnel when we die. He is also the friend who knows us inside and out better than we know ourselves. He is our Creator, and with the whole of His creation, we will stand before Him after we die. Because of the way

eternity transcends time, every single one of us will relive our
entire life then, standing more naked than we ever would be here
with all of our clothes off. Our every thought and feeling will be
publicly exposed.

I think we all tend to dismiss this scenario as unreal. If our faith
has any truth in it at all, however, everything will be more "real"
there than we can even imagine here. It is not that Orthodox
Christians believe in some horrible, punishing God. No, God
will not condemn us. If we are condemned, we will condemn ourselves. If we don't believe that, let us just look at our own fears. Look
at how we react when someone else suggests that we have made a
mistake or are less than perfect. Let us check out our own paranoia,
our own phobias. What will we do when there is no way to hide
them? How will we handle knowing that everyone without exception is facing us and suddenly knows everything we have ever
thought and said about them? How many of our thoughts and
actions will we be willing to take responsibility for? Where will our
virtue be then?

This is why the Church encourages us to practice, to prepare for
this entry into eternity. Role models for virtue are put before us in
the Scriptures, in the icons that surround us on the walls, and in the
lives of the saints, beginning with Jesus, the greatest model of all, on
down to the man or woman we may meet every day or every week
who shows us the secret of God's strength in daily life. We are taught
about individual virtues such as love, faith, hope, and purity in those
same writings. We have the opportunity to wrestle with our own
problems with these with friends, mentors, pastors, and guides. We
are given the chance to rehearse now in the confidentiality of sacra-
mental confession before we face the same confession in front of
everyone. And we should remember that the heart of confession is
telling what the Lord is doing in our lives. Even on Judgment Day,

we should be ready to declare the mighty works of God. Our con
fession should be of virtue, as well as of vice. We even should learn
to appreciate the chance for rehearsals when people accuse us of sins
and faults, whether real or slanderous. On Judgment Day, our enemies, both human and spiritual, will accuse us, showing our sins in
the most damning light. Then our salvation will lie in being able to
acknowledge them, take responsibility for them, and then to say:
"Lord, have mercy."

The Lord told us to win friends before that day. We are given
the chance to ask forgiveness of our family, friends, and neighbors
daily if we wish, or at least once a year in the Church as we begin
Great Lent. In liturgical services, we practice saying over and
over again those words that will get us through: "Lord, have mercy."
No justification, no excuses, no pretending or hiding. Just, "Lord,
have mercy."

If you are like me, you really need to practice saying this, since
it is not what comes first to mind when we are caught in a mistake,
let alone a sin. I have learned as a regular exercise to put myself
before the Lord in prayer and to look for the virtue He has planted
in my life. That is where real strength lies. Then, still in His presence, I can also go over some of the more painful and embarrassing
things in my life. We need exercises like this. We need to make
deliberate choices to cultivate the kind of life in which the God-
given seeds of virtue can grow.

Somehow all the excuses and justifications, and also the fan-
tasies about what I would want to do or would like to think I
am, look pretty flimsy in the presence of the Lord. At the same
time, the solid virtues that He has built into my life stand out. I
should give thanks for them, realizing that they are God's gift in
my life. I have no reason to boast of them—I know what I am like
without grace.

The battle for virtue is the reason for the time of Lent. This is the most important struggle of our lives. We need so badly to support each other in this. May God bless us all together in our journey to Pascha, both this year, and in eternity.

Chapter Seven

REFLECTIONS ON UNITY

S INCE I THINK WE TEND to use words carelessly, I began to look at what we mean when we use the word *unity*. It seems to me that for us today there are all kinds of unity. We can have a sense of unity with a whole list of very different people: old, young, well and strong, sick and handicapped, male, female, black, yellow, white, red, heterosexual, bisexual, homosexual, Christian, Orthodox, Jewish, Muslim, Hindu, Buddhist, atheist. With most anyone, we can find some bond. We can share a work environment, be in school together, live in the same apartment building, and be on the same sports team. We can share a cup of water, a loaf of bread, a glass of wine, a good meal, a good book, an intense experience. In fact, today in the United States, and at international settings such as the United Nations or the Olympics, if we refuse to "get together" in this way with any sort of group or person, at least on the surface, we can find ourselves in big trouble. In the global environment that is increasingly defining our culture, at least on the level of rhetoric, our common humanity is a given today. Many of us think nothing of this in every place—except in the Church.

This exception in the Church may be either a great relief or a great frustration to us. At work, at school, we may see real bonding among people from entirely different backgrounds. We may see people putting aside their differences for a common goal.

In our parish churches, however, we may instead see a group that defines itself by being different: We are Christians, not godless atheists, Muslims, Jews, or some New Age, "Eastern" religion. Further, we are Orthodox Christians, not Protestants or Catholics. Even more: Those of us who show up at things such as retreats, Bible studies, or mission vespers, are *good* Orthodox Christians, as opposed to the "nominal" people who come to church seemingly only when they feel like it.

But we don't stop there. Our parishes are often deliberately formed by people from a certain ethnic background (with a certain racial background being tacitly understood). We see that religion may divide people even within that exclusive group. Depending upon your generation or how your family understands itself, the language used, the clothes worn, the posture (when you stand or sit), the food you eat (especially at certain times and seasons of the year), all can divide. Even though others supposedly share our Orthodox religion, if they prefer pirogi to souvlaki (or never have heard of either one), or even share our taste for souvlaki or pirogi, but their accent indicates that they came from another side of the mountain, a different island, another tribal grouping, we know they will probably be more comfortable in another parish.

We find it easy to divide up our religion—to say there are many, different "orthodoxies": Greek, Russian, Antiochian, Albanian— even (perhaps) American. I have trouble with this term, "pan-Orthodox." Orthodoxy is one. The faith of the Church is one. Our God is one. Jesus Christ is not divided. We may be pan-ethnic, but please God, if we are Orthodox at all, we are decidedly not pan-Orthodox. We are called to find an even deeper unity in that faith than our secular brethren can find in the world, no matter how different our ethnic, family, educational, cultural, economic, or generational backgrounds may be. We should understand with our hearts, our souls, and even our "guts" that we are one here tonight in Christ. Christ's unity—the unity of the faith He gave us when He came to this earth as His Father's Word spoken to us in the flesh in order to die for us—this is what we are here to celebrate, even while we may very rightly glory in the diversity of our pan-ethnic make-up.

Orthodox Christian unity is given. It is given in the Body of Jesus Christ, crucified and broken—we choose whether to enter into it or not. Our church life, our personal lives either are formed by Christ, or they witness to some other reality that will not make it into the kingdom of heaven: Pilate and Herod found unity—became friends—by crucifying Christ. I've heard—and read—that people seem to think that was a good thing: Christ managed to reconcile enemies even at such a time. I think that is a very wrong interpretation. At compline each night at our monastery we sing from the prophecy of Isaiah: "The Lord shall destroy all who take counsel together." If, like Pilate and Herod, our agreement is our own, apart from God, it will lead only to our mutual destruction. All this means is that we will have company as we go to hell.

So what are we to do to enter into the unity of Christ? Should someone decree that at least here in America, OCA and Carpatho-Russian bishops serve only dioceses made up of people of Greek or Arab descent? Arab bishops lead the Russians? Convert bishops serve only cradle Orthodox, and Greek bishops serve only converts? Perhaps 30 percent of the parishioners from every Greek parish should be bused to an OCA parish every Sunday, 30 percent to an Antiochian parish, and so forth. Or simply mandate that every choir from every parish in a given area be on a traveling circuit, so everyone would get to hear some English, some Greek, some Ukrainian, some Slavonic, some Romanian, some Arabic.

Legislation like this won't work for us any better than it has worked for our country to heal the racial divisions or abolish crimes of hate, genocide, lust, passion, and envy. There is no real unity outside of the Truth. There can be superficial bonding and fellowship, but only those who want the kingdom of God—those who are willing to die to their own human limitations and preferences and allow the universal love of Christ to triumph in their lives—will find true unity.

We need to realize that on this earth perfect unity never has and never will exist. People are shocked to discover that there are divisions in the Church; that people in the Church, including bishops and clergy, can sin. We need to be reminded that the Lord's own handpicked group of twelve disciples was not a bunch of sweet petunias, and when James, Barnabas, and Paul were added to the mix, there were hot arguments and serious divisions. Honest struggle and even fighting can be, as St Paul says, the way to find the Truth. Or they may simply witness to the fact that the devil seems to be working the hardest these days in the Church, tempting and attacking everyone from the smallest child screaming and climbing around in the pews up through the middle-aged person who will come to church only if there is peace and quiet; to the choir interested mainly in the sound of their voices; to the burned-out priest who doesn't want to deal with any bad news; and finally to the bishop who wonders why on earth he ever got into his position.

We do need to remember that if our Church were organized according to the teaching of the apostles and fathers, such a term as "pan-Orthodox" wouldn't even exist. There would be no such thing as more than one bishop in one city; no parishes identified as anything other than the local Orthodox Church, the local Body of Christ. Period.

So what do *we* do? What *can* we do? How hard it is to accept the fact that we cannot save God's Church. God, through His Church, saves us. All our committees, our workshops, our plans will not and cannot achieve anything, as long as we think that we are the ones in charge.

A friend of mine often says that it is a form of insanity to keep doing the same thing and expect to get different results. We need to change, which is another word for the Lord's first gospel command to each one of us: "Repent." I cannot change anyone else, so here I will speak of what I know I need to do. I need to take time each and every day to remember deliberately and consciously that I am in the presence of God whether or not I am aware of Him (or even, as has been true at times in my life, whether or not I feel I believe in Him). I need to try to turn myself away from my own ideas, opinions, ways of doing things, at least for a few minutes every day in His presence, and ask Him to give me His thoughts, His ways. I need to admit to myself before Him that I am not perfect and that I am making a mess of my personal life and my public life and that I need His help. I need to bring before Him very deliberately all the people who are part of my life and to put aside my thoughts about them so I don't waste time telling Him what He already knows I think about them. Rather I need to let go of others, remembering that He is their God and they themselves stand, as I do, before Him. I think we all need to pray in this way. I need to pray for myself, for every sister in my monastery, for every member of my family, for those who work with me, for those who love me, and for those who hate me. All of you need to pray for yourselves, for every person in your parish church, for your priest, your bishop. We need to pray for other parishes, priests, and bishops as well. I believe our bishops and priests need to pray in this way for themselves, their people, and their parishes.

To learn to pray in this way—to learn to turn our lives and our churches over to God so that He can act—is probably the most difficult thing for Orthodox Christians to do in these days. We behave like functional atheists. We say we believe in God, but our actions show otherwise. We do not believe that He is the most important and most powerful Person in our lives and in the Church. If this is true, we are heretics at best, not Orthodox Christians, and we need to ask ourselves why we bother to come to church.

How many times have I heard Orthodox say: "I'm in church because my *baba* (or my *yaya*) was on her knees every day, praying for me"? Frequently they then go on to mention that their children and grandchildren no longer come to church. When I ask them if they get on their knees every day to pray for them, they often reply that no, that is not something they do; that is something their grandparents "used to do."

This is one of the reasons I think many of us today need remedial help to learn to pray. A wonderful teaching custom for those who haven't taken the first steps in learning to pray for others is this program that I saw enacted in a local Orthodox parish. After a Liturgy before Lent, pieces of paper were passed around on which everyone was to write their names. All the pieces of paper were put in a bag, mixed up, and passed around again. Each person pulled the name of someone else present, whom he or she was to secretly pray for each day through the whole of Great Lent. At Pascha, everyone was to tell their "prayer partner" who they were, greet them with the Paschal greeting, and give him or her a red egg. Everyone was also given a small card with a beautiful prayer to say each day for that person. When we are children in the faith, it is best to admit it and begin where we are.

As we do this—as we become praying members of the Body of Christ and through prayer give God even a tiny little space to enter into our lives and into the lives of our parishes—He can and will work wonders. Changes will take place. Even here on this earth, there will be moments when men and women will have real experiences of His unity and peace which surpass all our understanding. But as long as we insist on calling the parish we attend "our church," it will remain just that. We will be divided. Only God's Church, the Church of Christ, is one.

Chapter Eight

FIDELITY

"*H*E WHO IS FAITHFUL in a very little is faithful also in much; and he who is dishonest in a very little is dishonest also in much. If then you have not been faithful in the unrighteous mammon, who will entrust you with the true riches" (Lk 16.10–11)? The Lord's words are great ammunition to point at authority figures. As adolescents, we discover that our parents are not perfect, and we give enormous weight to their smallest sins. A parent who was mistaken about the clothes to be worn to a soccer game may then be seen as untrustworthy in every aspect of life. As adults, if we suspect government leaders to be less than perfect examples of private morality, we may likewise conclude that they are incapable of fidelity on any level. In the Church, we expect even more. Our leaders represent God on earth to us. We have a right to demand perfect faithfulness in all situations as the standard for their behavior.

Certainly there is truth to these arguments. I've learned, however, that looking at fidelity, as something I expect from others, is not a very practical—or Christian—way to live. In addition, judging others by my standards leaves me feeling angry and frustrated, since there is little or nothing I can do about the way others behave.

About the only thing I accomplish by judging others is to avoid looking at how I, myself, fail to measure up to those same standards.

Looking at fidelity from another angle, I've been touched by stories of men and women, who, hearing that their spouse or child had been lost in an accident or war, yet refused to lose hope. When they kept alive the possibility that their loved ones still lived, and went to heroic measures to find them or wait for them, and finally were rewarded by being united to them again, I am struck by the rightness of that resolution. On the contrary, when I've heard about couples or families broken apart by infidelity, I've felt something went wrong. The love must not have been strong enough, I tell myself.

Then we've all known people who are very warm and friendly with us. We feel their care when we are in their presence. We feel that they know what is best for us and can make sure that the best happens. If we only will let them take charge of our lives, we will have no more worries or cares. When we are young, it is good when our parents make us feel this way. Normally they are able to give us a needed sense of security for a while. But part of growing up is discovering that no human being has the ability to give us complete protection. Having grown used to some security as children, however, we often want it even when it is not truly possible. We normally go through a period of anger against all adults and authority figures, from God on down, when we discover that they are unable (or, especially in God's case, unwilling) to give us that protection, since they know it is not good for us.

How often anger is played out among us because we do not accept this reality. As adults, we may not want to give up the control of the life of another, even when it is obvious we can no longer exercise it. To accept that our actions need to change with the changing needs of others is a sign of true maturity. We may be angry when we discover that some person or group no longer provides us with the care and attention we have come to expect. When this care and attention is no longer appropriate, however, both sides need to change that relationship and get on with their lives. This is not infidelity; this is maturity. And when it is accepted, paradoxically it leads to a much deeper bond between people, even while externally they may not appear to be as close.

Yet doesn't this go against the Christian approach to relationships? Aren't marriages made to be indissoluble? "What God has joined together, let not man put asunder," said the Lord. Is not parenthood as eternal as God through whom we learn what it means to be a parent?

Christians would say, "Yes." Unfortunately, however, our experience of marriage and family life is often so limited that we do not know how to make room for the normal growth and development that people go through on their way to Christian maturity. A parent whose own needs have not been met, for example, will often try to hold on to his or her children in the name of "keeping the family together" long after it is appropriate. Such a person is asking for a false fidelity, and the result is usually the opposite of what is desired. When the children have been well nurtured early on, they may grow beyond their parent's own level of maturity and be ready for the next step. It may in fact be a compliment to their father or their mother that they no longer need the attention and care required by a child. If the parent still needs that relationship, however, and will not accept anything other than immediate closeness and dependence, the child may feel driven to break parental ties completely.

Likewise in a marriage, when either or both of the partners grow beyond their immediate need for close physical and emotional dependence—when the honeymoon is over and the annoying differences appear in greater relief—many people begin to look for the magic again elsewhere. Little do they realize that they are short-circuiting the deepest and most fulfilling part of a relationship.

True love begins between spouses, between parents and children, between siblings, between friends, and in monasteries between community members only when our love no longer primarily fulfills our own needs but rejoices in the growth and well-being of the others.

This is how God loves—and it is not an easy way. For us humans by ourselves, in fact, it is impossible. A family or monastery that does not understand this is doomed to dysfunctional failure. Without a faith that inspires each person to build a relationship with God in as concrete and daily a manner as every other relationship, mere human relationships will fail. In truth, we need to become aware of the way God loves us in order to learn how to love others. Only He can be truly faithful and meet our needs fully.

Often I refuse to see that He does this. I do not accept that He knows me better than I do. When He allows pain and disaster to touch my life, I have been known to feel that He has abandoned me. I am too weak to suffer in that way. I want to remain a small child held by the hand and carried over life's rough spots.

I come by this honestly: American society is built largely upon the efforts of men and women to remove the rough spots, to improve upon God's approach. We may even be willing to suffer ourselves, but we become righteously indignant when we see others suffer. Perhaps we accept it when they suffer through the results of their own foolishness, but when they are innocent victims, especially of "natural" disasters, we feel that if there is a God, He must at best be indifferent or at worst vindictive.

When I feel this way, I tend to measure myself as well by my ability to keep those around me from suffering. When I cannot, I feel like a failure. I may go to great lengths to protect those around me from the consequences of their own bad choices and find myself angry with them when, rather than showing gratitude, they resent me and exhibit increasingly outrageous behavior. When this begins to happen, a warning signal should go off in my brain. I must immediately stop looking at the situation and at others. I must instead turn within and check on my awareness of my Creator. Do I see that He is present? Am I willing to address words to Him whether or not I can say I am consciously aware of His presence? This can be the brief act of faith that is so famous in ascetic literature but so difficult to act upon. After all, it means admitting my inner poverty and my powerlessness. It may mean physically walking from a room, taking a moment to be still and to pull myself together. Even worse, since God is present in such moments whether or not I am aware of Him, He may well allow me to see my own wrongs, failures, and limitations. Eventually, He may also bring me to the point where I realize I can and must change and acknowledge this to others. This small act of turning to God is the most transforming and powerful tool in my life.

When I don't want to change—when I would rather spend time mentally cataloging the wrongs of others so I can feel good about myself instead—taking a moment to pray in this way can seem incredibly difficult. I may prefer to put in hours of hard labor at almost any other task. Yet this is where I must begin if there is going to be any change in my life.

St Seraphim of Sarov said, "Acquire the Holy Spirit and thousands around you will be saved." I cannot save those around me; only God can. Until I take this first step in prayer, I cannot expect Him to act with power in my life. When I do not allow Him to open the doors for change in my own life, how can I expect any change around me? There is no other way, and each of us must walk it. What a joy it is to discover that others walk it as well! May God, who alone shows us true fidelity, continue to transform His Church from within, beginning with me and with you. Amen.

Chapter Nine

PHILANTHROPY*

*T*HERE ARE TIMES when it seems as if we cannot truly love people and also love God: People have too many needs; they are too demanding. If one is called to love God with all of one's heart, soul, and strength, what is there left over? Yet, reading the Scriptures and listening to the teachings of all those who have spoken of God through the ages, we know that we cannot truly love God unless we love our neighbor. It is not an "either/or" proposition, but a "both/and."

Jesus said: "You shall love the Lord your God with all your heart, with all your soul and with all your strength and with all your mind, and your neighbor as yourself" (Lk 2.27).

"He who does not love his neighbor whom he has seen, cannot love God whom he has not seen" (1 Jn 4.20).

The Lord has told us that what we do to the least of our brethren we have done to him (cf. Mt 25.31–46). When a man went to the great Pachomius, founder of communal monasticism in fourth-century Egypt, and asked to be shown God, St Pachomius took him out to the garden and showed him an old, dirty, and not very pleasant

---

*July 1996. Written for the International Orthodox Christian Charities (IOCC) program booklet, reprinted with permission.

monk. He then told the man that if he could not see God when he looked at this monk, he would not see him anyplace else, either.

St James tells us in his epistle that our faith and our love must further prove themselves by action. "You say you have faith? By my works, I will show you my faith!" "If you say to a poor person with nothing, 'Go in peace, be warmed and filled,' without giving them the things needed for the body, what does it profit? So faith by itself, if it has no works, is dead" (Jas 2.16–17).

An old nun once told me that the whole point of the monastic life was to learn to love even when it isn't easy. Men and women enter a monastery to learn to love God by loving and serving their brethren in difficult situations. They do not choose one another for romantic interest or because of family or social ties; they cannot get away from each other by going off to work or going out to social events; they cannot escape from each other and from their life together before God by watching television or hopping into the car to drive around for awhile or hang out with more congenial friends. And they must learn to listen to one another and try to fulfill the needs of their brethren, no matter how difficult or unpleasant this may be.

This is the most basic part of *philanthropy,* a word coming from the Greek *philanthropos*, meaning "a lover of mankind." Without this struggle to love and serve others, anything we may like to call love for God is merely empty words or sentiment. Further, as St Paul tells us, even if we are very generous with our goods, even if we give our body to be burned, if we do not have this love, our efforts count for nothing (cf. 1 Cor 13).

Yet when we come to see God in our neighbor, when even a little of God's grace allows us to experience the love that God Himself has for His entire creation, then we find ourselves searching for the innumerable ways before us that allow us to give generously of our possessions, our time and effort, our very being. We come to realize that our neighbor is our self. We come to feel deeply that our own greatest good is served when we serve God through our neighbor.

And we learn "to put our money where our mouth is." We find ways to give our abundance to help the poverty of others. St Paul tells us not to give voluntarily to the point that we ourselves will be in such poverty that we will need the help of others, but if we have an abundance, when we love, we will want to share.

Americans living in the United States have often had little experience of poverty and suffering. They often find it hard to believe that others could need desperately the amounts they spend having "fun." Yet even in the United States, there is growing poverty. In addition to the poor and the homeless, philanthropic institutions both within and outside the Church, seminaries, monasteries, and other such places find themselves struggling to survive. Those in this country who have given their whole lives to the service of God and His people—in organizations such as the International Orthodox Christian Charities (IOCC), or as missionaries, and even as monks and nuns—often know that the money to pay for groceries for the week is not in the bank and also know others with families who have not had such money for an even longer period. They often do not have enough to share themselves, yet often they have the incentive to find ways of helping in spite of that.

How difficult it can be at times for such people to listen to the conversation of well-meaning visitors who exclaim over the good work these people are doing and shower them with compliments. Often, then, such people will hand them a "generous" gift of ten dollars, while talking about their latest vacation trip to an exotic place or the expensive clothes they just couldn't resist buying. They seem to believe that they "need" all these things. And truly, there are times when something seemingly frivolous is life-giving therapy for an ailing person. Yet the money saved by giving up even just one vacation trip one year and doing instead some activities with family and friends at home could save the lives of several children both here and abroad. Or it can give parents the tools and training they need to work to support them and their families. Or it can enable organizations to survive and grow so that their members will continue to pray and work for others without further compensation.

Let us pray that God will give us the grace to learn to love one another in deed as well as in word and intention, for then and only then will we truly come to share in the life of Him who is known most truly as the Lover of Mankind, the greatest of philanthropists.

Chapter Ten

A QUESTION OF LOVE

*H*OW DOES ONE ATTEMPT to love God and neighbor as an Orthodox Christian? In my own experience, the words of St John the Theologian, especially in his First Epistle, ring very true: "In this is love, not that we loved God but that He loved us and sent His Son to be the expiation for our sins. Beloved, if God so loved us, we also ought to love one another. No man has ever seen God; if we love one another, God abides in us and His love is perfected in us" (4.10–12).

Again, quoting the Lord in the Fourth Gospel: "He who has my commandments and keeps them, he it is who loves Me" (14.21). If we ask what His commandments are, we again have His words: "A new commandment I give to you, that you love one another as I have loved you" (13.34). Likewise, He prayed for us to His Father, saying: "I made known to them Your name, and I will make it known, that the love with which You have loved me may be in them and I in them" (17.26).

Our very being and life and our ability to love come from God. It seems to me that the most important step in learning to love is to turn to this God who has made us and ask Him to open our eyes to the truth of love. For there are as many false ways of loving as there are false gods in this world. As Orthodox Christians, we know that our God is fully manifested to us not in laws or canons or regulations or church services, but in the person of Jesus Christ and in the members that make up His Body on earth, the Church. So to turn to God means to turn first to Jesus and take the first steps in prayer.

Although He was fully God and from our perspective perhaps should not have needed to do so, Jesus took time for such prayer. As Man, He knew He needed consciously to put Himself in a place—away from the distractions of other people and the events of His life—where He could become aware of the presence of His Father. "And in the morning, a great while before day, He rose and went out to a lonely place, and there He prayed" (Mk 1.35). How much more we need to do this if our love is going to be true and life giving.

We must learn to ask God in prayer to reveal Himself to us and not only to show us His love, but also to fill us with it. As creatures, we are bound to Him for eternity, for we have no life apart from Him. If we find that such a thought is a problem for us, we need to struggle in prayer with ourselves and with Him about it. For apart from Him, we can do nothing, including loving.

Most of us have witnessed at one time or another people caught in a relationship they call "love," which is nevertheless tremendously destructive. Both feel that they "need" the other person so much that they must constantly keep them in their control to fulfill this need. The other person is not seen as a free creature, beloved by God, but as a possession to be used. God may well seem to be a threat to those in such a relationship. For God's love teaches us to let go and to give the other freedom. When we serve them, we must do it for love of them and not to control them or get a reward of any kind. How hard this is! And yet that is how God loves us. So often, in the name of "love," we want to "play God" in the lives of others in a way that He does not.

So to learn to love, let us learn to pray. Let us learn to find others and ourselves in God and allow Him to give them life and love. Let us come to see that we are bound in this great love of God with the whole of creation. True love does not stop with those who are useful to us. Let us come to respect all people as friends as well as lovers, and care lovingly for the small planet given to us in the midst of the vast reaches of the universe. Then we will find the love that has reached out from before time and eternity and holds us in its embrace. Here even in our sins we may experience this love from time to time, "laying aside all earthly cares" and turning to the source of love. Let us gradually let His love so fill us that we can return it to Him through others. There is no other source or way.

Chapter Eleven

SPIRITUAL GROWTH IN

A WORLD OF TEMPTATION

*E*VEN A TERM AS commonplace as "spiritual growth" may mean
different things to different people. I will begin by defining
what I think it means.

First of all, there are many, many spirits. I want to be quite clear
that for myself, the only spirit I want to be interested in is the Holy
Spirit of our Lord God and Savior, Jesus Christ. And I know that for
myself, the only real way to enter into that Spirit is to enter into
Christ's own life. There are many ways that Christ has given us to do
this, and Jesus shows us the ways: prayer to God, offering Him worship in the service that is His due; reading and taking to heart the
Bible and the writings of the saints of the Church; and learning to
respect as well as to love those around us, wherever we may be. Certainly any retreat on spiritual growth should include time to reflect
on how each one of us will make these ways our own.

When we enter into Christ's own life through such means, God
gradually begins to live His own life in us as well. Then we grow, not
in the spirit of a Pharisee, or the spirit of a New Age cult adept, or
some other lesser spirit, but we come to the spirit of participation in
God's own life: *theosis*, to use the Greek term. St Peter speaks of this

in his Second Epistle (1.4). St Seraphim of Sarov told his friend
Motovilov that the whole aim of the Christian life was to acquire the
Holy Spirit. This is what I mean by spiritual growth.

As Orthodox, at least once a year, we are used to hearing a ser-
mon on the parable Jesus told of the Publican and the Pharisee. This
is not a bad thing, but I have observed an interesting phenomenon
that sometimes results from it. The fathers of the Church and the
liturgical texts for that Sunday point out that the Publican was not
justified because he was a sinner, but because he repented. Likewise,
the Pharisee was not condemned because he fasted, tithed, and
lived a moral life, but because he condemned another person. At
times it seems, though, that the prevailing spirit tells us we should
feel the sinner is blessed just because he is a sinner and that anyone
who tries to live a moral life or grow as a Christian is necessarily a
hypocritical Pharisee.

This is a very subtle, insidious point. It is amazing how subtle
alien spirits can be and how quickly we can exhibit such unhealthy
spiritual growth. Of course, there is the other, very obvious temptation to fall into: a variation of the sin of the Pharisee. It is so hard to
avoid that one! We manage a little virtue, we stand out a bit from the
secular crowd, and rather than comparing ourselves to God and realizing that compared with all He does for us—not to mention the fact
that we exist solely through His life-creating power and mercy—that
we are, in Jesus' words, merely unprofitable servants who have only
done our duty, we begin to fancy ourselves as pillars of the Church
and role models for all those around us. We instantly get the warm,
rosy glow that comes from the sure knowledge that spiritually we
have grown to be a few inches taller than the other people we see.
And, of course, then we are dead in the water.

So this spiritual growth is to be approached with great caution
and not to be hastily identified. The same is true of the "World of

Temptation" around us. An elderly nun once said to me that she thought most people misunderstood the true nature of the worldly spirits we are to avoid. She said she felt the real spirit of the world was a spirit of despair, a spirit of hopelessness, a spirit of judgment and condemnation. She said she worried more about women who brought such a spirit into the monastery than she did about the so-called worldly women who knew how to rejoice in the goodness of God's creation. God did not send His Son into the world to condemn the world, but that through Him the world might be saved. We are called to see Christ in and through the whole of creation, and St John in his First Epistle even goes so far as to claim that our love for God exists no more and no less than the love we have for our brother. I heard this paraphrased once as, "We love God as much as the person we love least." The Lord said that hell fire is reserved for those who call their brother a fool. How easy it is to fall into such a spirit and in the name even of spiritual growth, see evil in all those around us. "To the pure, You show Yourself pure, but to the crooked You show Yourself shrewd" (Ps 18.26).

I fall into this worldly temptation. I just need to look around the church and see all the people who hold different opinions from my own very solid and sane grasp of the truth. One of my big temptations comes when we attend parish liturgies, and it becomes obvious to me that most of the people there don't know that when we Orthodox are at the Divine Liturgy, we are not just spectators or pew potatoes, but members of the royal priesthood of Christ, all of us concelebrating with the priest. We have no more right to sit through parts of the service than he does. We are there to work along with him at this great service of worship and praise that is due to our God. This is why Orthodox churches never had pews until the Orthodox came to America and saw what all the Protestants were doing. To me, it is obvious that people have given in to this worldly temptation. They wanted to fit in and be American like everyone else; therefore, they took the model of the all-American Protestant service where the minister preaches, and the organist plays, and everyone else is just supposed to sit and listen enthusiastically. Even though the Orthodox might not have understood what they were doing or why, because it was all in a language they did not understand and no one explained it to them, still, they were doing something—and as every sports or fitness enthusiast can tell you, just doing something active is enough to get your endorphins going so you feel good. If you don't understand what is going on and you are also just sitting there being bored, there is absolutely no chance for you to have any positive feelings about the experience of "going to church" on Sunday morning. No wonder we lost a whole generation before English services came in.

As you see, I feel very strongly about this, and I am obviously right. Just as I feel strongly about my obviously right attitudes toward the questions of old versus new calendar, contemporary versus archaic or foreign language, whether or not married clergy should dress like monastics and women should cover their heads, whether or not we need more than one seminary in the Church (and if so, which one?) . . . the list is almost endless. All of these are burning issues, and I would love to start a party platform, induce someone to run on my ticket, and start a large party organization with fundraisers, speeches, and rallies.

But the Lord (not to mention St Paul and millions of other saints) is pretty clear that such a party spirit is from the world of temptation. As Americans, it is so ingrained in us that we don't even see it most of the time. We root for Holy Cross, St Vladimir's, or St Tikhon's exactly the same way we root for the Pittsburgh Steelers or the Democrats. Perhaps it is harmless when we root for our favorite sports team (depending on how obsessed we get about it and whether in practical, everyday life, it becomes much more compelling than God's reality). But such a spirit is never harmless in the Church, and it is one of the greatest hindrances the world places in the way of our spiritual growth—not to mention the growth of our badly divided parishes and jurisdictions.

So in the name of growing spiritually, let us not just sit around exchanging Lenten recipes so that we can diet properly during Lenten periods, discuss the merits of our obviously superior favorite monastery or spiritual father, or exhibit the latest fashions in prayer ropes. Rather, let our growth consist in learning, if we don't know, how to treat even the brothers and sisters we disagree with the most with courtesy, respect, and love. May we learn to listen to even the least of God's people and certainly to hear the truth of the words of St John Climacus, who wrote: "Let us who are weak and passionate have the courage to offer our infirmity and natural weakness to Christ with unhesitating faith, and confess it to Him; and we shall be certain to obtain His help, even beyond our merit, if only we unceasingly go right down to the depth of humility" (*The Ladder of Divine Ascent* 1.8).

I suggest, my brothers and sisters, that this is the only spiritual growth worth having in this very fallen and sinful world of temptation.

Chapter Twelve

THE SLAVERY OF THOUGHTS

OF MY OWN MAKING

O NE OF THE CLASSIC disciplines of monastic life has been to learn how to "guard one's thoughts." This expression can be found throughout the writings of the desert fathers as well as in later writings of ascetic elders and guides down to our own day. We read in the lives of many of the saints that they lived closely with such guides and elders in sketes or monasteries until they had learned to watch their thoughts, and then they were blessed to go out into the desert as hermits to fight the devil and his armies.

There are many levels of "guarding one's thoughts" in this tradition. There is the basic struggle to get control of the process of thought itself, using a prayer such as "Lord Jesus Christ, Son of God, have mercy on me, a sinner." For longer or shorter periods of time, normally set with the direction of one's spiritual guide, one continually repeats such a prayer, setting aside all thoughts as they appear, good or bad, and turning to the Lord in simplicity and purity of heart.

Then there is the struggle in periods of temptation, when evil thoughts and passions fill the mind and heart. Again, one uses such prayer to turn to the Lord. In these struggles, especially against evil thoughts and passions, the ascetic fathers and mothers insist strongly that we are not to try to fight thoughts and passions on our own, for we will be defeated. But we are to call upon the Lord, who alone can destroy the powers of evil, and to allow His presence to drive them away.

There is another level, however, on which I believe we must also struggle to master our thoughts: to think rightly. These are the times when we cannot try to put aside all thought in prayer but must use our minds to work by God's grace, to make decisions, and to plan.

I was given a very practical example of this struggle as a youngster in monastic life. With my fellow novices, I was told of an old monk who had been greatly loved and respected by his monastery. He kept a notebook in which he carefully recorded the times when his assured judgment had been proven wrong. We read some notes he had written at his brothers' request, in which he said that he considered that notebook to be one of his greatest treasures. I remember both being very struck by that and also thinking what an odd thing it was.

At that time, I was fresh from the American school system of the fifties and early sixties. If there was one thing I had been taught, it was that my own thinking, unhindered by faith or the heart, should be my most trustworthy guide. We were all told many times that the whole point of education was to teach us to think. If we were tested and found to be wrong in our thinking, terrible things happened.

And tested we were. Nearly every day the results of our thoughts and reasoning, right or wrong, were tallied up and held in front of our eyes and the eyes of our classmates and peers. If not immediately, then periodically, our parents and families were also shown whether or not we could prove we were right. To be able to do this well was the ticket to our future: to schools, jobs, marriage with a person who also had this coveted ability to be right in his or her thinking so we would perpetuate this in our children. We also were being trained to add to the vast body of correct facts that our society began collecting once it had realized that objective truth could be measured and tested in the name of science. The myths of earlier generations were being exposed. Those who lived in the modern world, unlike all previous generations who had ever lived on the earth, by having access to the facts through right thoughts and reasoning unsullied by the human heart or by faith, could be freed from myth and falsehood and live lives based on reality.

Creating such a climate of right thinking for the world was an awesome responsibility, and our poor brains were sorely taxed. A book called *Water Babies* by Charles Kingsley was required reading for a course I took on Victorian literature. There was a garden in the story, as I recall, with talking turnips and radishes, and from time to time one of them would burst open. Kingsley's characters were informed that these had once been children, and education had left them with nothing but their unsupported, ever-swelling heads. I remember the flash of recognition: "That's me!"

Formed both by this system of education and by the very different approach to life found in the Church, I have found myself confronted by other struggles as well. It seems at times as if I am at least two different people. The main person, the one I call myself, raised from childhood as a Christian, believes with both my heart and my mind in Jesus Christ as the God-Man, our Lord and our Savior. There seems to be another part, however, far more influenced by those years of classroom education when our minds were, in effect, trained to work in isolation from the rest of our being. This part of me can be bombarded by all kinds of thoughts that are "in the air" today. While the rest of me protests, it can have thoughts that span practically every heresy ever condemned by the Church. Today,

I would say that part of me was trained to think even apart from "common sense."

The "educated" thoughts this part glibly has accepted have proven false in so many life situations over the years, however, that it is not hard to dismiss them. Naïve assumptions, gained in the fifties, of how nice the world was becoming, for example, simply have not been able to stand up to my own experience and the experiences of so many of my friends, new and old: lives marked by abuse, not to mention the continuing and sometimes even escalating horrors of poverty, war, and terror both at home and abroad.

Through such gained experience, I have come to know that truth is not manufactured within my own mind but is God-given. When we take times regularly to open our minds and hearts to God in prayer we discover a unity of truth the fallen world cannot begin to understand. When the heart (which the tradition of the Church understands as the center of our being) is purified through prayer and a life of ascetic discipline, it has eyes that perceive deeply and truly. When through this same process of prayer and ascetic discipline, the mind and heart begin to work together, our whole being is informed by truth, love, and revelation. Then our minds find peace, insight, and discernment. In fact, we begin to think clearly and rightly, perhaps for the first time. Rather than struggling, we are challenged by eternal delight. We begin to find that our thoughts and perceptions do not deceive us. When united with the heart, they find enormous joy both in discovering the intricacies of the world and universe created by God and also in joining with the Church to sing of the great condescension of our incarnate God and the divine transfiguration of our humanity in the risen and ascended Christ.

This is an important way of disciplining our thoughts; of understanding words such as those found in a traditional, post-communion prayer to the Theotokos: "Grant me a release from the slavery of the thoughts of my own making." Our own fallen thoughts can in fact become evil and misguided taskmasters leading us into deadly, eternal bondage, if we do not take them under control and guard them through prayer. They rather control us, keeping us trapped and limited. We are not able to bring our minds into our hearts to find mental, emotional, and physical wholeness.

On the level of daily life, if we do not engage in this struggle we will tend to trap other people as well in our fallen thoughts. If our brains have been told, even unconsciously, to generate "correct" thoughts or opinions about others, we will continually study them, analyze their words and behaviors, and come to conclusions about them and the "kind of persons" they are. Often, again unconsciously, we will do this so that when we are around them we will be able to behave in ways appropriate to them.

This, however, is a fallen human approach. We should learn rather to suspend judgment. We should begin to pray for others, and then our minds will begin to see clearly the mystery of life unfold in them. Insofar as we are able, we should treat them with unfailing love and respect, no matter how they have treated others and us in the past. This can be very difficult. In fact, God, who pours out His love on all mankind, no matter what kind of people they may be, is the only one able to do it perfectly. While we try to keep others in the molds we have formed for them, so that our hard-won opinions about them will continue to be correct, He, at every moment, continues to pour out on them with great generosity all that is necessary for their eternal life and salvation.

For us to make even a start at such a God-like approach, let us take times when we suspend our thoughts, no matter how correct or true they may seem to be, and remind ourselves that God's reality is as far beyond their comprehension as heaven is above the depths of the sea. Let us take time to turn to God and to call on Him as frequently as possible, using the words of whatever prayers help us to do this.

Let us guard our thoughts and come to have a healthy distrust of the thoughts of our own making. Let us also learn to treasure up the times when our seemingly assured judgment has been proven wrong. Let us rejoice as we learn to see God's reality more clearly with both our mind and our heart. Let us come to seek the mind of Christ, and to know that our whole being already has been found in Him. Only then will we begin to know the truth and reality that exist in love with God and with our neighbor.

Chapter Thirteen

CLIMBING THE SPIRITUAL LADDER

E ALL KNOW THAT we are living in a rapidly changing culture. The one thing certain is that nothing will stay the same for long. Concepts such as God, eternity, heaven, hell, and prayer, which reflect unchanging realities, are very foreign to most of us. Even those of us who have been brought up within a churchly environment, where we've been made to feel comfortable with eternal truths, may feel as if we are split personalities as we go about the business of our daily lives.

Obviously the Church, as we experience it through its members and institutions, is also affected in greater or lesser degrees by this same split personality. Gone are the days when living a Christian life could be seen as simply the normal way for a citizen to function. Once again, Christians are faced with the reality of two citizenships: one allied to the state and society, and the other allied to the very different citizenship of the Church.

In all honesty, probably the two citizenships were never quite as wedded as we like to think. The Emperor Constantine certainly changed the way Christians perceived themselves, but we know that his acceptance of Christianity as the state religion also brought many difficulties. It can be an easy way of excusing ourselves to say it was easier to be a Christian "back then," whenever "then" may be. I would

like to submit, however, that if our God is the eternal Being we know
Him to be in Trinity and through His self-revelation both through
His Spirit and His Word in Jesus Christ, we have no excuses. On
Judgment Day, we will be expected to have lived as Christians, even
though we have come of age in the twentieth century.

Our task, then, is to work within the time and place we have been
given. This is not an easy approach to the Christian life when it is
done with integrity. I have chosen the image of the "Spiritual Ladder" made popular by St John Climacus, because I think it is a useful tool for us in this task. The ladder rungs are the same for us as
they have been for Christians down through the ages. Even more,
the top of the ladder is placed at the same goal Christians have
always struggled to reach—that of love. What differs for us is where
we find this ladder and how we begin to climb it. I would submit that
in the same way the Gospel teaches us we must carry our own cross,
we also must climb our own ladder—not someone else's.

St John tells us in his classic exposition of the Ladder that we all
must begin with the first step, "Exile." Obviously this was something
of a struggle for the monastics for whom he initially was writing:
leaving their families, their jobs, and the comfort of their private
security. Yet all of us need to make a conscious choice if we are going
to make the Christian faith our own. As more than one person has
pointed out, all of us who are in the Church as adults are converts.

Yet what does this mean? Ours is not the first generation to have
large numbers of people reject their own society and look for enlight-
enment primarily in foreign and exotic cultures. Even those who
choose to come to or stay within the Church often take this same
route. God certainly can work with such an approach to exile when
it is undertaken with sincerity and purity of heart. Yet I think there
is another way. We do not necessarily need to change our clothes,
take a new name, buy ethnic cookbooks, or learn new languages in

order to follow Christ in our generation. And those of us who have come to this country from foreign lands with a Christian culture do not necessarily need to remain within our ethnic ghetto to maintain our faith and to grow in prayer.

I would submit that the Eastern churches have an excellent foundation for those of us who are working to place our spiritual ladders and begin climbing—not just because of our great traditions such as monasticism, hesychasm, our beautiful liturgical services and vestments, our saints and martyrs, but even more because of the very many faithful men and women who live ordinary lives in the world: attending public schools, taking part in sports and the other social events of American culture, and holding jobs up and down the ladder of the American economy.

These are the people who are in the advance guard of Christ's army on earth—not the professional religious people such as clergy and the monastics. We have our role, but let's face it: We are the ones who live in the shelter of the army camp, with plenty of supplies around us, sheltered from the front. We do see the worst the enemy can do, since those who are injured in the battle of life often end up at the doors of our tents with gaping wounds of body and soul in desperate need of healing. Yet our main task is to keep the home fires burning, to provide places of refreshment, inspiration, and recreation for those who are sent to us. How understandable that many of them fall by the wayside in the midst of the terrible battle of this life—how less excusable when we are not faithful, surrounded as we are by the strength and power of our Lord. How terrible when some of us even become the enemy within the camp.

We religious types can be subtly tempted to become the enemy to our fellow Christians. It can be easy to forget the parable of the Publican and the Pharisee. How easy it is to decide, for example, that those who do not have an Athonite spiritual father (Optina fathers being extinct), do not attend every church service and Bible study, and do not openly wear their prayer ropes are not as spiritual as they should be. I have heard people speaking this way and it appalls me. I often wonder if such people have read the Gospels. Theirs may be a form of spirituality, but I am not sure it is a Christian one.

Then how, in this busy world of ours, do "ordinary" people pray? Where do they find their ladder? Can those who are not able to spend long hours "paying attention to God" in prayer and religious exercises still become saints: men and women of prayer?

I would say definitively, "Yes." To understand this, let us remember that our relationship with the Lord has often been compared to that of a husband and wife. At the beginning of such intimate relationships, time is needed to become accustomed to the beloved. The courtship and honeymoon phase of marriage are proverbial for that kind of close attention. Yet normally, a marriage moves beyond the need for such constant, physical closeness. A couple learns to feel they are married; act in a way that is appropriate to married people, even when they are apart and getting on with the business of their lives that frequently separates them for long periods of time.

Even more than a marriage, our life in God comes to encompass everything we are and everything we do. We cannot exist, speak, or act apart from Him. That is a fact, whether or not we are ready to accept it or act upon it. In a sense, it is very simple. If Christians take the time to remind themselves of that fact, even briefly each day, the rest of their lives gradually begin to fall into place. I would submit that this is the heart of exile and the most basic part of prayer: to acknowledge that we are in the presence of God, to learn to turn to Him, speak to Him, and then to be silent before Him so that He may speak to us. All of this can be done within a five-minute period, so there is no excuse for not taking such time. And many, many so-called common people in our parishes are doing just this.

Having said that, as with any relationship, there need to be times when we work harder on being in the presence of the Beloved. There need to be times when we spend more time in our icon corner, stay in God's house, sing songs of praise and worship, study about Him, fast, make serious choices about our priorities, pray with others, and get the support we need from the Church to carry on the rest of our lives, knowing that all we do is in His presence.

We all need to learn that we can pray when we are doing other things. While we do need to take time to turn to Him—to give Him at least the basic courtesy of a greeting every day, and more if our lives and our circumstances allow it—if we do this type of simple prayer with sincerity and a whole heart, we will find that we become gradually aware of Him no matter where we are and what we are doing. To send a quick thought, an inward nod of the head so to speak, in His direction, can keep us centered in the midst of all sorts of distractions. The apostle Paul tells us to pray without ceasing, yet we know that he was a man of immense activity.

We also need help with the thoughts and feelings that bombard us both from outside and within our own heads and hearts. The fathers and mothers of the Church tell us that we will never get away from such thoughts and feelings; they always will be there. This is again where simple prayer, a verse from the Psalms, "Lord, have mercy," the Lord's name—whatever seems right for us—may be used, almost like a tennis racket to bat the distracting feelings and thoughts away. As long as we can do this—as long as we can separate ourselves from them for even a brief moment—we are not held captive by them. That little space we create each time we "hit" such a thought or feeling with the name of the Lord or some other brief prayer, gives God all the room He needs to act in our lives. We simply learn not to be bothered by the fact that thoughts and feelings are there.

Many people also find themselves feeling that the official prayers of the Church are sometimes too long and wordy. I would submit that there is nothing wrong with such a feeling. There are people who do really like long prayers—the more elaborate the better; the more obscure the language the better. There are other people who simply can't pray that way. Or if they can at first, they soon find it becomes impossible for them. Even in church, during longer prayers, they find themselves unable to concentrate. This has always been true. Not every one is called to pray in the same way. There are gifts that vary here, as well. For many of us, the same prayers we teach our children to "get by heart" will continue to be the best prayers for ourselves: to turn to God with simple words such as "Our Father," or "Holy God, Holy Mighty, Holy Immortal, have mercy on us." Or, our own words telling Him our troubles, our joys, our private thanks and requests, and asking Him to take care of us and our loved ones— this can be the highest form of prayer for many people. We should realize that if prayer is something other than turning to God, it has lost its meaning and purpose. Just to "say prayers," or "use the Jesus prayer" in such a way that we are more aware of ourselves praying than of being in His presence, is a waste of energy. As our Lord said, "Not everyone who says 'Lord, Lord,' will enter the kingdom of heaven."

Even this simple prayer can be a major struggle, however. We must not underestimate what those around us may be going through when they seem to do no more than appear faithfully in church on Sunday. This is a fallen world. The devil has a vested interest in keeping us unaware of God's presence. What should be simple can begin to look like a horrible task. In truth, there are some teachers who do make prayer a "burden too hard to be borne." There are people who are called to be the Olympic athletes of prayer—to read long Scripture passages and whole prayer books through every day; make hundreds of prostrations; take on severe fasts; attend every possible service; spend at least an hour each day in silent meditation. There are others like the Publican who are called simply to live their whole lives before God in humility and love. A heartfelt "Lord have mercy on me a sinner" is all we need to be justified before Him. Some of us need to admit that we aren't given the gifts or the providence for the "Olympic" kind of prayer and get on with our lives, turning to God as we can through the day, not beating ourselves up because we aren't as good as the Pharisee.

By now you may be wondering about the "Jesus prayer." Many people today seem to believe that it is the only truly "Orthodox" prayer. Yet this is not accurate or traditional. The prayer of Jesus mentioned in early writers such as St John Climacus was actually the Lord's Prayer ("Our Father . . ."). We need to remember that in the gospel accounts, when the disciples asked Jesus how to pray He did not tell them to use the Jesus prayer. Some people find it is a good tool to use to turn to the Lord; let Him be the One who fights off the distracting thoughts for them. Others find other words more useful—or even turning to Him without words. If we call on the Lord using His name, we also need to be sure that we know who He is. I'm more than a little concerned by people who use the Jesus prayer without knowing the Gospels—without even having read the New Testament through once. Who is the Jesus they are praying to? The Jesus prayer is not a magical incantation. He certainly is able to work in spite of our ignorance. But not many of us are illiterate peasants, unable to read and ponder His Word in the Gospel. We will be called to account for the use of our gifts and talents. If the ability to read is one of them, then we should do just that to inform our prayer. St Paul again tells us to "pray with understanding."

We all need to be reminded of the importance of what we are doing as Christians. A large part of the job of professional religious

people is to equip others for the battle. It gets down to what we
believe about God. Are we functional atheists? Do we say God is all-
powerful, but really think we are the only ones who can do anything
important? If God is who we Orthodox say He is, then turning to
Him through our tasks, during our conversations, is the only way to
gain a real perspective on what we are doing. When we lose that
sense of an "upper level" in our lives, we lose the ability to think
clearly and with compassion. We are no longer living as Christians.
If we understand that, then the problem of "making time for prayer"
ceases to be a problem. We will see how we are without Him, and we
won't want to be that way. We will find that even when there are
emergencies when it is obvious we must serve our neighbor in immediate need, we can grab time "on the run" as it were. We must be careful to remember that He loves our neighbor more than we do. Often
we need to realize there is no emergency we need to take care of;
we're just busybodies. If we do our own job, live our own lives, and
put our loved ones into His hands, they have a much better chance
of learning to stand on their own feet and living their own lives
before Him as well.

I do think that many people are tempted to make prayer and the
Christian life much too exotic and complicated. We don't want just
to climb a ladder—we want to do acrobatics and tie ourselves up in
knots. Our Lord became incarnate as a very commonplace person,
not even as exotic a figure as St John the Baptist. He came simply to
give us abundant life in our circumstances here and now so that we
will also find it in eternity. He did not mention spirituality. He did
not present prayer as an end in itself. We need to do what we can,
not what we can't. I think many of the people in our churches who
don't pray have been led to believe that the only way is to take lots of
time, read lots of books, use fancy words. They know they can't do
that, so sometimes, it is true, they do nothing. We should let them

know that there is another way and that it is a very traditional one. Simple, heart-felt prayer is something anyone can do at any time. If we are called to do more by our gifts and situation, then God will bless us—only let us not attempt more without guidance or we can become judgmental Pharisees rather than men and women of deep and compassionate love and prayer. The Lord said something about becoming like little children in order to enter into the kingdom of heaven. St John Climacus puts it another way—we can't climb the whole ladder in one leap. We must be willing to take humbly the first step that is presented to us in our lives.

Chapter Fourteen

CHRISTIAN SPIRITUAL MATURITY:
BEYOND THE BASICS

L ET US DEFINE MATURITY as open-ended, eternal growth into all the fullness of God. Let us also say that the Church provides us with tools we need to nurture and encourage that growth. Today, in the Lord's providence, we are familiar with many such tools. Many of us can pray in church as St Paul recommended, understanding the words of Scripture, hymns, and sermons in our own language (1 Cor 14.15). Many of us can attend Christian education classes, retreats, and study groups. All of us, if we so choose, can avail ourselves of the many books, periodicals, tape recordings, and videos available today through mail order sources, even if they are not available in our local parishes.

Yet I would submit that necessary as these tools are for us, especially today, they bring us only to the very beginning of our journey into Christian spiritual maturity.

What else is needed? The answer is simple: the desire, the will, and the effort to encounter the living God in prayer.

How do we gain this desire, will, and effort? We cannot gain them on our own. They are God's gifts. Yet He gives His gifts to all who ask (Lk 11.10–13) and normally through the regular give and take of life. We need only to respond to the slightest stirrings in our hearts.

How do we respond? First of all, our fallen human nature is forgetful, and we will need to remind ourselves that we are always in the presence of the God who is everywhere and fills all things. For this, we will need times of personal prayer, apart from the worship we offer God in church. In addition to praying with heartfelt desire and honesty during our crucial first moments of waking and final moments before sleep, we will need to seek out other times of silence when we "lay aside all earthly cares," all external stimulation and noise. This is how Christians from all walks of life have taken seriously Christ's call to "enter your closet and shut the door" (Mt 6.6) for at least two obvious and important reasons: to clear away distractions so that we can attend to the "one thing needful" (Lk 10.42) and to stop running away from ourselves.

For much, if not all, of our human lives can be spent paying attention to everything and everyone except that which we can do something about: our selves. First, however, we need to place ourselves in God's presence, for only as He allows us to see more clearly in His light and with the eyes of His love, may we safely begin to look at ourselves without either false vanity or shame and despair. Only then may we hope to begin to look at the people and situations around us without annoyance, offense, anger, or perhaps lust or desire for control; for only then can we see how much God loves every one of us in complete freedom in spite of who we are.

A normal outgrowth of such quiet times of prayer, however briefly free from noise and distraction, is the desire for even more silence. It is usually possible to be creative and find times, ways, and places to work, relax, and re-create away from the world's noise. When it is not, we can ask God for the grace to create and enter into a quiet space within ourselves. Daily burdens, stress, and

physical, mental, and emotional illness can make even this difficult
or at times impossible. Still, our Lord God and Savior Jesus Christ
has told us that His Father will always give the Holy Spirit to those
who ask (Lk 11.13). There will always be some times when we can
experience the inner peace that is God's gift.

As we grow in familiarity with silence and the inner peace that
comes from God, we will find ourselves with the ability to walk a bit
faster along the path of life. For one thing, we will gradually discover
a growing ability to listen, which is the basis of obedience—a virtue
for all Christians, not just monastics (cf. Rom 1.5, 5.19, 6.16, 16.26;
Heb 5.8; 1 Pet 1.22). We will discover that even conversations and
meetings need not be exercises in noise and frustration when we take
moments of silence to digest and reflect on what we have heard.

Yet when we are alone, we may at first find silence much more
difficult than cultivating moments of quiet in conversation with others. We may discover that inwardly we are a crowd of people shout-
ing a chorus of worries, cares, and woes, making up scenarios for our
next social encounters, rehearsing lines to rebut or entertain possible
or imaginary audiences, and so on. How do we live with this and still
find real silence?

Experienced ascetics tell us that we will never get away from
being bombarded by such inner noise from our own thoughts or
those of the devil and the fallen world. Today that is especially true,
when subliminal background noise is constantly being programmed
into us. Nevertheless, we can use brief words of prayer to "shoot
down" thoughts so that we don't totally identify with them.

The saints of the Church tell us further that it is necessary at
times to "shoot down" even our seemingly good thoughts as an
important regular exercise. When we practice giving up our own
thoughts and words, even as on occasion we lay aside our own way
of doing a task, we become more able to hear clearly when others

have different ways of thinking and of doing things. This is also a form of sacrifice. In the Biblical, Christian tradition, to sacrifice means (literally) to make something holy—by giving it up. (We are also to give up things that are bad, not as sacrifice, but as common sense!) When we sacrifice and give up good things, God takes them and makes them holy, and in a mysterious way, returns them to us purified and stronger (Mt 19.27–29). If He doesn't send them back to us in that way, the wisdom and experience of the Church teaches us that they weren't as good as we thought they were, and we are better off without them (cf. 1 Cor 3.13–15).

Preachers, teachers, iconographers, writers, poets, musicians—indeed people from all walks of life—have told of preparing for their words or work with prayer and then discovering that their task "takes on a life of its own," entirely different from their own original ideas. Some of this may be the simple mechanism that results from the deeper intuitions and thoughts of one's subconscious surfacing as one puts aside one's more conscious "bright ideas." Yet the Lord has also told us that God's Holy Spirit is able directly to inspire His creatures through this same process: "Do not be anxious how you are to speak or what you are to say; for what you are to say will be given to you in that hour; for it is not you who speak, but the Spirit of your Father speaking through you" (Mt 10.19–20).

The next part of obedience that we will develop is the ability literally to be "response-able." For in a sense, we all listen; we may just listen more to ourselves than to others and to the reality God sends our way. As we become better listeners to voices other than our own, as we become more aware of reality outside of ourselves, we can begin to respond to others and to our situation more appropriately.

As we find we are growing more comfortable with the ways of obedience, we may begin to want a spiritual guide, friend, or mentor. If God wants us to have such a person in our lives, we can be sure he or she will appear. We must beware that we don't miss the lessons we can learn from others, however, just because we don't think they are as holy or advanced as we are. It has been pointed out that if God can speak through Balaam's ass, He can speak through the most unlikely persons and situations, if we have the eyes to see and the ears to hear. If God wants us to learn obedience in the normal ways, putting aside our self will by being appropriately obedient to those around us—such as our spouse or other family members, our parish priest, other members of our parish, those at our work or school— and by prayerful reading and study of the Lord's example and guidance in the Gospels, then it will be safest for us to follow that route rather than looking vainly for a relationship God may know would bring us only to vanity and delusion.

If we continue humbly, accepting the obvious guides or lack of guides God allows us in His providence, we will slowly become more aware of ourselves as others see us. This can be devastating, and we ought not to seek such awareness, or force it on others, before the right time. All of us will have many "moments of truth" when we are confronted with the opinions of others, whether or not we want to be aware of them. Here again, our growing sense of God's presence and love for us is crucial. Only He can look at our worst sins and corruption, our biggest mistakes, errors, and self-imposed limitations with complete and unconditional love. When others see us, and when we see others, we are still too blinded by our own sins and fallen nature to see beyond these things (Mt 7.1–5). If we could see clearly as God sees, we would find it impossible to dislike, judge, or hate anyone, including ourselves (1 Jn 4.20). As it is, we humans find the total acceptance we need only from God, even though He may choose to show it through others.

Nevertheless, we know from the Lord's own example that there are times when we ought not to trust ourselves to the opinions and manipulations of others (cf. Jn 2.24–25 and Lk 4.29–30). We should learn not to take seriously the counsel and criticism of others, however helpfully intended, when they themselves are not open to counsel or criticism, lest, as St John Climacus points out, we "mistake the sick man for the doctor, the sailor for the ship's captain and so bring our ship to wreck in the harbor." This is a matter for great prayer and discernment, however, for there is also a saying that he who is guided only by his own advice is guided by a fool. Especially when we are not being asked to compromise either our Orthodox faith or our morals and ethics, it is critical for us to hear what others have to tell us, even about ourselves, and to have the freedom to follow their directions. We know we are growing when we can begin to face the facts and truth that others tell us and can at times do things their way without anger, frustration, or discouragement.

Laziness, compulsive behaviors, addictions, bad habits of word and deed—we slowly begin to become aware of these and other faults in ourselves where before we had noticed them only in others.

When we are willing to persevere through this, after the first layer of unpleasant garbage has been washed away by the clear water of the Holy Spirit entering the stagnant cesspool of our lives, we may find ourselves on a very pleasant stretch of life for awhile. Those who know us may see that we have changed and that we are nicer to be around. This is normal. It is a sort of "honeymoon" that God may give us to encourage us at the beginning of our walk with Him. In ignorance, we may be tempted to think that we have reached full maturity.

Soon, however, we will discover that we have many more layers of dirt that missed that first washing. We may feel that we are never going to be clean. Then, again bit-by-bit, we may start feeling a little better: Our families and friends can see that we aren't leaving such a muddy trail behind us. They know and understand how far we have come and tend to be appreciative and supportive.

So another stage of our journey may coincide with a physical move to another place, making new friends, getting a new job, entering a monastery, or having another similar life change. Here no one knows our past; our good deeds and progress are not interesting. We have to start all over again to rebuild our good reputation. If we have gradually come to think of ourselves as nice people, we may startle even ourselves by the anger we feel when others do not recognize our spiritual worth. We may be tempted to think that they are bad people who cause this anger within us. The truth of the matter is no one can make us angry or behave badly unless we choose to let him or her do so. Anger can be accompanied by feelings of loneliness and discouragement, but these are simply natural parts of growing up.

Along with this growth in obedience and the humility of self-knowledge, God will allow our progress to be tested with some real misfortunes, tragedies, and setbacks. If we are relying only on ourselves and our own strength, we will be thrown back again and again into our feelings of despair and discouragement. When we finally learn our limits and weaknesses from these experiences and let them prompt us to turn more fervently to God in prayer, we will begin to gain strength even from adversity, and the devil will not be able to "rejoice twice." We will fear neither adversity nor fortune, for we will know that any virtue we may have comes not from our own efforts but from God alone.

The true Dark Night of the Soul, or final purgation mentioned in ascetical literature, is reserved for those who persevere, gaining love, joy, strength, and stamina from their journey. Probably most of us will never really get to this point in our lives here on earth. If we have allowed God to fill our lives to the brim with His love; allowed the fire of His cleansing Spirit to burn out all our dross and temper our gold; faced the worst pain, terror, and loss the world has to offer, then possibly if God so wills, we may be called on to enter in some way into the darkness Jesus Himself faced on the Cross, when having fulfilled all righteousness He yet found Himself crying out, "My God, my God, why have You forsaken me?" This was not a cry of despair. It was the voice of God's human experience, entering the lowest depths of the fallen human state cut off from the Father, so that even in His presence we sense only abandonment. The writer of Hebrews (4.15) wrote: "For we have not a high priest who is unable to sympathize with our weaknesses, but one who in every respect has been tempted as we are, yet without sin."

In His infinite wisdom, God perfects some people who seem to have spent their lives in sin, degradation, and hurtful violence, by placing them at the moment of death in the presence of a forgiving love that transforms their end. Or at the end He may put them through all of these stages of Christian maturity, including the "Dark Night" of the soul during one brief episode of illness, persecution, torture, or other great suffering. Others who have lived good lives may be perfected through a long and lingering illness, suffering from something like Alzheimer's disease, which strips them of any responsibility or virtue they seemed to have gained. God leads us each in a unique way. What seems to be the end here is merely the door opening onto an eternity of growth into love and life.

If we do nothing else then, let us turn to God in love and trust, saying to Him with all the heartfelt sincerity we can muster: "Let Your will, not mine, be done." Let us throw ourselves, like little children, into the arms of His mercy, there to find the true maturity, which alone can lead us into the kingdom of heaven (Mk 10.15).

Chapter Fifteen

CHRISTIAN OBEDIENCE:

BEYOND THE BASICS

*O*BEDIENCE HAS FALLEN on hard times. While the word is still used by Christians, it is rarely understood in a healthy manner. To most people it means surrendering all responsibility for actions and behavior. Either they believe that no one in their right mind should do this, or they embrace something like a cult, believing that giving up all responsibility is the only way for Christians to act.

But does true Christian obedience mean surrendering responsibility? We know from looking at the English word *obedience* that it comes from the Latin *obaudire,* which means "to listen well." Many languages do not have separate words for listening and obedience. Only as English speakers have lost touch with the roots of their language have they gradually slipped into this separation and misunderstanding.

Let us look at the results of this misunderstanding and see if there is not another way to approach the whole subject.

I believe that the most obvious result of our culture's misunderstanding of obedience is the breakdown in relationships. Because we may rightly fear such giving up of all personal responsibility, we have an unconscious aversion to getting close to almost anyone, knowing that, rightly or wrongly, obedience is at the heart of relationships. We fear that our God-given selves will be threatened by others; that we will not be able to grow into our God-given gifts and potential if we live and work closely in contexts such as marriage, family, parish, or monastery. I think this helps to explain the statistical explosion, even for otherwise practicing Christians, of live-in relationships without commitment, often accompanied by inhuman work schedules euphemistically referred to as careers or professions.

But is it true that committed relationships limit our growth and personalities? Are we deformed by sacrificing for the sake of others some of the ways we might use our gifts and talents? Is the choice to give up a pet dream, in order to make time for work to help support a family or community, necessarily deadening? Or on the other hand, is setting aside a career in order to have time to raise our children or care for our elders necessarily less self-fulfilling? Is putting ourselves under monastic obedience the end of our God-given personal growth and creativity?

I would say "no" to all of these questions. As Christians, we believe that God calls each one of us into being and by this creating call wills us to live and work in a community of love. Any tasks we may perform, any words we may use, any attitudes we may hold, are sterile at best if we see ourselves fulfilled in isolation. As human beings, we are made by God to be capable of growing into our full potential only in communion with others. We know that this is critically true of infants, who will die from lack of simple human attention, even if they are given adequate food and shelter. It is true also of adults who believe they have reached a level of maturity where they no longer need others. Their self-chosen tasks, whether practical or artistic, can lead to ultimate insanity and death if this course of isolation is uncompromisingly pursued.

Yet how do we work out our salvation in communion with others? How do we avoid the pitfalls of isolation on the one hand and abusive, destructive relationships on the other?

I believe that we begin by learning literally to repent and to obey. The English word *repent* in Scripture translates the Greek word *metanoia*, which means "to change one's mind (or heart)." According to our faith, to grow into the fullness of being means an eternity of such change and growth from the fallen human nature we inherit into participation in the fullness of God's own nature. This was the first call of Christ when He began to preach: "Repent and believe in the Gospel" (Mk 1.15).

In this Biblical sense, repentance and true obedience go hand in hand. We must listen in order to hear the word of repentance.

Perhaps, then, the best working definition of obedience for us today is responsible listening. Through the obedience of responsible listening we begin to learn our limitations as well as our strengths and potential. However, listening does us no good if we do not respond appropriately. I would submit that true Christian obedience is a dialogue. All persons involved in obedience must listen and respond appropriately. A husband or wife who makes demands without seeing or listening to the needs of the other spouse or family members becomes a tyrant and abuser rather than the head of the household. The same is true of a monastic superior. Members of a family, a monastery, or a parish should not exist only to fulfill or serve the needs, desires, or whims of the person with some kind of authority. Christ came not to be served but to serve (Mt 20.28), and we can have no greater authority than His.

Since my own experience of obedience has been gained within the monastery, I will write of that experience. Because it seems that the nature of obedience is the same in both monasteries and families, I trust that what I write will also make sense to those who are not monastics. Those who through circumstances or choice are not members of either a family or a monastery may need to be more creative in discovering their own obedience, within a parish or other church family, at work or with neighbors. Each of us needs to learn to listen and respond with our head and our heart together.

For a monastic, the obedience of responsible listening and responding appropriately begins before entering the monastery. A person may perceive a call from God. Such a perceived call should always lead to repentance and newness of life. But in the beginning, we never fully understand the direction to which God is calling us. In *The Ladder of Divine Ascent,* St John Climacus tells us that this is a blessing—if we could see the trials and difficulties ahead of us, we would never begin (Step 1.24).

In addition, he tells us that when we are seekers, we have vices and pride that need correction. Therefore we must "test, as it were, the superior," before placing ourselves under obedience to him or her, so that we do not mistake a sick man for a doctor, or a sailor for the pilot of the ship (Step 4.6). For most of us, this means first visiting several monasteries to get a perspective on the life and on those who will be guiding us in it. We need to ask questions and think things through. We should be looking for a monastery where we will be supported in a lifetime of repentance. We also need to understand that those responsible for the life of the monastery will be asking questions and thinking things through with us as well.

It is not inappropriate to ask at least as many questions as we would ask before taking a new job. We should assume nothing in the beginning and seek advice from others as well as making our own observations. We should look at those who have been formed by the life of the monastery over a period of time. Are these people who can lead us by precept or example? We should talk with those outside who are familiar with the monastery; check its references, as it were, just as we can expect our own to be checked. We need to be able to trust and talk openly and freely with those who will be responsible for our souls. Does the person who will be our mentor listen to us and respond appropriately to our questions? Does he or she in turn ask questions to learn about us?

How we approach our entry into monastic life (or marriage) may lead to success or failure. We should realize that the commitment of a lifetime needs a well-built foundation. In St Luke's Gospel, we hear the Lord telling us that we should be "like a man building a house, who dug deep and laid the foundation upon rock; and when a flood arose, the stream broke against that house and could not shake it because it had been well built" (Lk 6.48). Later in that Gospel He speaks again about preparation: "Whoever does not bear his own cross and come after me, cannot be my disciple. For which of you, desiring to build a tower, does not first sit down and count the cost, whether he has enough to complete it? Otherwise, when he has laid a foundation, and is not able to finish, all who see it begin to mock him, saying, 'This man began to build, and was not able to fin- ish.' Or what king, going to encounter another king in war, will not sit down first and take counsel whether he is able with ten thousand to meet him who comes against him with twenty thousand? And if not, while the other is yet a great way off, he sends an embassy and asks terms of peace. So therefore, whoever of you does not renounce all that he has cannot be my disciple" (Lk 14.27–33).

It is interesting to see that in St Luke, the ability to bear our own cross and renounce all that we have is equated with having the resources to begin a new endeavor. Indeed, this is at the heart of obe- dience. If we begin any undertaking, great or small, simply by reck- oning up our own natural gifts and talents or the possessions and wealth we may have acquired, we will not achieve anything great for

the Lord. We must be willing to surrender all that we are and all that
we have, to spend and be spent. Again in St Luke's Gospel, we find
Jesus saying to all, "If any one would come after me, let him deny
himself and take up his cross daily and follow me. For whoever
would save his life will lose it; and whoever loses his life for my sake,
he will save it. For what does it profit a man if he gains the whole
world and loses or forfeits himself?" (Lk 9.23–25).

In whatever we undertake, our first obedience must be to Christ.
We need to ask His guidance through prayer and searching the
Scriptures, taking His words to heart before we begin our journey. If
we read and re-read the Old and New Testaments with prayer and
try to understand words such as *obedience* from their context, rather
than simply reading in our own contemporary misunderstandings,
we may be surprised at what we find. The same will be true as we
read the other Christian writings: the sayings of the desert fathers
and mothers, the classics of St Basil the Great, St John Chrysostom,
and St John Climacus, down through the writings of the saints for
two thousand years into our own times. A good guide will question
us about our reading and point out references we might well miss on
our own as we lay our foundation in obedience.

We in monasteries who mentor women and men seeking to test
their vocations must likewise cultivate honesty and awareness. We
should not lead people on when we know our monastery cannot
meet their needs. Perhaps we can help them find another monastery
better equipped to handle their special gifts and talents as well as
their limitations, or perhaps we should help them accept another
direction in their lives.

If we are in a position of authority, we need to be aware that not
everyone will be able to trust us and work with us. We are not God,
and if we sense that a person does not respect us and the authority
we represent, we should not take them on as members. They cannot

~~grow without the respect and trust in their mentors that alone lead~~
to responsible obedience.

Because respect and trust normally take time to develop, a quick "love at first sight" relationship may be superficial at best, and certainly needs to be tested. Both superiors and candidates (and couples in love) may be unaware that what seems to be openness and candor can hide unknown depths. Very few people are given the gift of complete self-knowledge. We are all wounded, and God knows that we can come to see our fallen selves only gradually. The deeper the wounds and hurts, the longer will be the healing process. When major surgery is required for complete mending, the patient usually needs a long period of time to get in shape for the procedure. In my experience, the people with the deepest wounds may look the nicest on the surface: They may not even realize the extent of their inner damage and turmoil. They sense only a great need to keep up a pleasant exterior, and that absorbs all of their energy.

A truly healthy person in this fallen universe is not free of troubles and illness, but rather has the awareness necessary to use the medicines and therapies appropriate to his or her situation. A monastic superior should rarely, if ever, try to take away such medicines and therapies. It is true that a person ought not to continue the use of crutches after healing has taken place, but an outsider can rarely have the intuitive knowledge to discern when that moment has come. The best we can do is question and encourage—and accept that there will be some people whose illnesses are too severe to be handled with our monastery's resources. God has other plans for them.

This process of discernment at the start of a person's monastic vocation is critical if obedience is to be freely given. If obedience is forced, if a person's responses to what he or she hears are based on fear rather than freedom and love, a faulty foundation has been laid.

A critical time always comes for such a person when the reason for this fear has been removed. Someone may eventually perceive, for example, that they *could* survive as a Christian in the world; that they will not be damned to hell if they leave the monastery. This is a common reason why many people suddenly leave the monastery even after many years, with little or no warning—especially those who have outwardly appeared to be very "obedient," always doing as they were told without questioning or complaining. If there had been more dialogue, if someone had known their thoughts and difficulties, if their obedience had literally been more "response-able," they might have had the freedom to choose monastic life again on a solid basis when their fear left them.

St Benedict, a sixth-century monastic guide who lived in the West yet drew on the wisdom of the Eastern desert fathers, sets out some definite guidelines for obedience within the monastery, once the discernment has been made that a person should enter and test his or her vocation. He states that the abbot or superior shall do nothing without taking counsel (*The Rule*, chapter 3). He further states that if the superior asks someone to take on a task, if that person believes the task to be beyond their capabilities, they should say so, with all respect and courtesy (*The Rule*, chapter 68). This is absolutely necessary for responsible obedience. We may know something our superior does not know, and if we withhold this knowledge, then the failure of our task lies with us, not with those who have asked us to perform it. On the other hand, others may see strengths and potentials within us that we cannot see ourselves. Very often, after hearing the objections of a monastic, a superior may nevertheless encourage the person to try a difficult task. If we trust our superior, we may well discover gifts we had not realized we had. And even if the task is beyond our best efforts, we (and our superior) will have learned something, both about the task and about our own limitations. Thus obedience can also lead to true humility, the greatest gift of Christian life.

Especially at the beginning of our monastic life, before we "know the ropes," in addition to voicing our doubts and objections, we need to ask further questions about our obedience. Does the person giving us our task (who may not be the superior of the monastery) want us to go ahead on our own, finding and using the appropriate tools and procedures? Or does she or he want us to work under direction, using recommended procedures and tools? If we want to learn the ways of the monastery and learn to work with our sisters or brothers, we should be ready to accept either approach. As adults, we should realize that obedience is not a power struggle between two people, but rather a dialogue by which the will of God is discerned in things both small and great.

On the side of those in authority, those who direct or give tasks to others in the monastery must make sure that the resources of time and tools are available. Miracles can and do happen when monastics obey impossible requests out of humility, love, and trust. Nevertheless, we must be sure we would be willing to follow a direction ourselves before we give it to others. If we have not proved that we can be obedient, how can we even know how to ask such obedience of others? In such an atmosphere of understanding and trust, all those living within the monastery, superiors and others, will find themselves challenged to grow beyond their self-imposed limitations and grow into the fullness of their God-given potential.

It should be obvious in this setting that superiors cannot claim to voice the will of God and speak in the Holy Spirit if they are unwilling to listen. They may need to make unpopular decisions, but when they believe that is necessary, they must be very certain that they are basing decisions on more than their knowledge. The greater the decision, the greater will be their need for counsel. If the decision will affect the ongoing life of the monastery, then they need to hear the thoughts and feelings of every person in it, including the most recent arrival (*The Rule*, chapter 3).

While their own obedience does mean that they are to make the final decisions within the monastery, if they do not make them in an appropriate way, responding to situations and people first with listening and prayer, those decisions will be to their condemnation. They need to remember that the monastery is not theirs, but God's, and that the salvation and welfare of fellow monastics is their priority, not their own needs and wishes. They need to maintain a healthy balance between the needs of the sisters or brothers, both as individuals and as a group, and the work necessary to maintain the functioning of the monastery. The superior and his or her fellow monastics also need to remember that the superior's own needs must be cared for, however, or she or he will not be able to be fully present for others.

In a monastery, as in a family, a parish, or other church organization, wonderful, blessed things can happen when each and every person listens and responds appropriately to what is asked of them. Truly God is in the midst of such a place, and there are no limits to what can be done in love for His glory and for the salvation of all mankind.

LET GOD ARISE!

Let God Arise!
Let Him laugh as He rolls
      this small marble of earth
      from its orbit.
Let men clap their hands
      to see stars turn to dust
      in the light of His face—
the word that gives meaning.